T0381181

When Docker Meets Java

A Practical Guide to Docker for Java and Spring Boot Applications

Ashish Choudhary

Apress®

When Docker Meets Java: A Practical Guide to Docker for Java and Spring Boot Applications

Ashish Choudhary
Pune, Maharashtra, India

ISBN-13 (pbk): 979-8-8688-1299-6   ISBN-13 (electronic): 979-8-8688-1300-9
https://doi.org/10.1007/979-8-8688-1300-9

Managing Director, Apress Media LLC: Welmoed Spahr
Acquisitions Editor: Melissa Duffy
Development Editor: Laura Berendson
Editorial Assistant: Gryffin Winkler

Cover designed by eStudioCalamar

Cover image by Markus Kammermann from Pixabay

Distributed to the book trade worldwide by Springer Science+Business Media New York, 1 New York Plaza, Suite 4600, New York, NY 10004-1562, USA. Phone 1-800-SPRINGER, fax (201) 348-4505, e-mail orders-ny@springer-sbm.com, or visit www.springeronline.com. Apress Media, LLC is a California LLC and the sole member (owner) is Springer Science + Business Media Finance Inc (SSBM Finance Inc). SSBM Finance Inc is a **Delaware** corporation.

For information on translations, please e-mail booktranslations@springernature.com; for reprint, paperback, or audio rights, please e-mail bookpermissions@springernature.com.

Apress titles may be purchased in bulk for academic, corporate, or promotional use. eBook versions and licenses are also available for most titles. For more information, reference our Print and eBook Bulk Sales web page at http://www.apress.com/bulk-sales.

Any source code or other supplementary material referenced by the author in this book is available to readers on GitHub. For more detailed information, please visit https://www.apress.com/gp/services/source-code.

If disposing of this product, please recycle the paper

To my daughter Viya and son Ayansh, who fill my world with joy and wonder.

To my wife Shefali, my unwavering partner and source of strength.

To my parents, for their endless love and guidance.

This book is for you.

Table of Contents

About the Author

 **Ashish Choudhary** is a senior software engineer and published author. He has over 14 years of experience in the IT industry. He has experience in designing, developing, and deploying web applications. His technical expertise includes Java, Spring Boot, Docker, Kubernetes, IMDG, Distributed Systems, Microservices, DevOps, and the Cloud. He is an active blogger and technical writer. He has delivered talks at renowned conferences like GitHub Satellite India and Fosdem. He is a strong advocate of open source technologies. He has been contributing to various open source projects for quite some time. Ashish believes in continuous learning and knowledge sharing.

About the Technical Reviewer

 **Anant Chowdhary** is a software engineer working on bringing AI-based dubbing to videos. Having completed a master's in Computer Science with a focus on Machine Learning and Distributed Systems, Anant is a technology professional with extensive experience in designing and optimizing complex systems. He is deeply interested in the transformative potential of emerging technologies, particularly AI and automation, and how these innovations are reshaping industries, society, and the way we interact with the world.

Passionate about exploring the intersection of technology and human behavior, he is committed to understanding the broader implications of digital advancements on both individuals and communities. Working on planet scale systems, he has a wealth of experience in Distributed Systems and Applied Machine Learning.

CHAPTER 1

Overview of Containers

As a child, I spent so much time using Lego to build things, all the while thinking that there was no way these stupidly simple and standardized 2x4 bricks could be the origin of all the awesome possibilities. Little did I know that those colorful blocks were instilling in me the fundamental principle of modern software development. Just as Lego reinvented play, containers have fundamentally changed how we develop, package, and deploy applications. Now imagine your software as if it were a Lego construction. Containers are individual building blocks, standardized and endlessly combinable, each one representing a containerized component.

Just like the toy bricks, containers provide a standard way to bundle applications for portability across any compatible system where they run. Need to scale up? Simple: add more "bricks." Want to update a feature? Pop out one container and snap in another, without toppling the whole tower. Lego is magical in its modularity and flexibility: easily built, broken apart, and rebuilt. In software development, containers bring the same agility to software development. They isolate applications and their dependencies, just like individual Lego bricks are self-contained units. Such isolation ensures that just like a red 2×4 brick makes no difference whether it is in a castle or a spaceship, your application will be running identically whether it is on your laptop or inside a cloud data center.

In this chapter, we put the pieces of container technology together and explore how those digital building blocks have constructed a new era in computing. At the end of this, you're going to see how containers are the doors to innovation: making developers able to build, share, and deploy their digital creations with unimaginable ease and creativity.

© Ashish Choudhary 2025
A. Choudhary, *When Docker Meets Java*, https://doi.org/10.1007/979-8-8688-1300-9_1

A Bit of History

In 2010, a small startup called dotCloud was struggling in the competitive Platform-as-a-Service market. What they didn't know was that they were actually about to change the tech world.

Headed by Solomon Hykes, the dotCloud team developed an in-house tool for managing Linux containers that were meant to improve their system but soon became so much more.

Linux Containers are a kind of operating system-level virtualization, running multiple independent Linux environments on one machine. LXC shares the host machine's kernel with each one, which gives a leaner alternative to a virtual machine, yet maintains process, file system, and network space isolation.

LXC utilizes cgroups (control groups) and namespaces to manage and limit resources, producing a virtualization experience similar to running natively on an underlying system without the overhead of a full hypervisor.

Hykes introduced Docker at PyCon in March 2013. He received an immediate and enthusiastic response from the developers because Docker suggested a solution for how to more easily create, deploy, and run applications consistently in any environment.

A key innovation in Docker was its capability to bundle an application and its dependencies in a standardized unit, that is, containing libraries, dependencies, configuration files, and runtime environment—in a consistent format, which is also called a container. This alone solved the age-old developer headache: "It works on my machine!"

As Docker became popular, dotCloud shifted direction. They renamed it to Docker, Inc., and now focused exclusively on creating the Docker ecosystem. The project gained momentum very quickly:

Docker Hub was launched in 2014, providing a central location for images of containers.

In 2015, Docker Swarm followed with the native orchestration of containers.

Docker Enterprise Edition was released in 2017 to suit the needs of businesses.

Docker was a total shift in software development. It made containerization and microservices architecture more popular and drastically changed how companies develop and deploy applications.

It was not always smooth. Docker, Inc. had financial difficulties that forced it to sell its Enterprise business in 2019, although the core Docker technology remained very influential.

Today, Docker is at the heart of many development workflows. This story exemplifies how an internal tool can become an industry-shaping technology through the uptake and contribution of an open source community.

As we explore containers throughout this book, we'll learn about the story of Docker in the background. It's a reminder that radical solutions have humble beginnings, and when the timing is right, they have the power to transform whole industries.

Definition of Containers

Let's begin by exploring a formal definition of containers before going deeper.

Docker's Definition

Docker defines container as follows:

A container is a standard unit of software that packages up code and all its dependencies, so the application runs quickly and reliably from one computing environment to another. A Docker container image is a lightweight, standalone, executable package of software that includes everything needed to run an application: code, runtime, system tools, system libraries, and settings.

Understanding Containers

This definition provides a more comprehensive and easily understandable explanation. For a Java application, the container will encompass the base image, JRE (Java Runtime Environment), application code, and other necessary dependencies for its execution.

Let's further illustrate this concept with an additional example. In Java, a Class serves as a blueprint or template defining the state and behavior of objects. By utilizing this template, we can create multiple instances of the class. Similarly, a container image is a template from which numerous container instances can be generated.

Containers can be compared to black boxes without their internal details being visible. Each container possesses its own IP address, hostname, and disk. While we will explore the benefits of containers in future lessons, isolation is one of their notable advantages. Consider running two applications requiring distinct versions of Java or incompatible tools and libraries. Achieving this on virtual machines (VMs) would be challenging, resulting in resource wastage. However, such isolation is inherent with containers, and running multiple applications with different requirements becomes feasible.

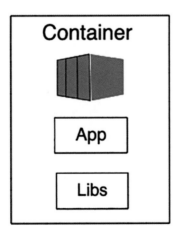

Figure 1-1. *Container*

As illustrated in Figure 1-2, the accompanying image, the underlying infrastructure, represented at the bottom, can be a physical machine or a VM. On top of it lies the operating system layer. The container engine is responsible for running containers on the host machine. At the top of the image, we observe two separate applications running inside individual containers, each wholly isolated.

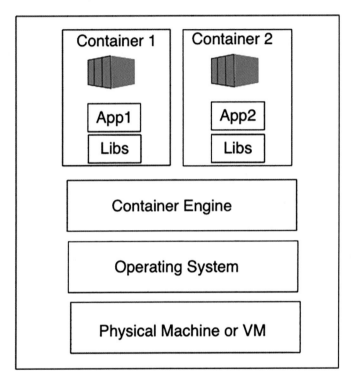

Figure 1-2. *Visual representation of containers*

Let's understand more about containers with an analogy.

- Imagine Java containers similar to JAR (Java Archive) files. In Java programming, a JAR file encapsulates Java classes and resources into a single file, making it convenient to distribute and run applications.

- Now, picture containers as a broader concept that operates similarly. Like JAR files, containers package an application with its required dependencies and configuration files. This encapsulation ensures the application runs consistently across various environments, from development to production.

- It's similar to placing our Java program and all its dependencies inside a single, self-sufficient container, ensuring seamless functionality no matter where we put it. In this analogy, just as a JAR file contains compiled Java code and resources, a container houses an entire application with everything it needs to operate successfully.

Containers encapsulate required dependencies, functioning as self-contained entities with IP addresses, hostnames, and disk configurations. The container engine executes them on the host machine. These containers package an application with essential dependencies and configuration files, ensuring consistent functionality across various environments, much like JAR files.

The Significance of Containers

According to the 2023 DZone Containers Trend Report, containerization continues to mature and usher. Moreover, container adoption is increasing, particularly in large businesses, as most large organizations are going through digital transformation to enhance their IT and business capabilities. The point is there are some apparent benefits of containerizing our workloads.

So, what's this fuss about containers, and why should we adopt containers in our organization?

Key Advantages of Containers

Containers offer several key advantages that make them a popular choice in software development and deployment.

Portability

Portability in computing refers to the capability of executing a computer program or software on an operating system different from the one it was initially designed for. Due to their inherent portability, containers can be utilized across various platforms. They are compatible with Linux, Windows, macOS, and numerous other widely used operating systems, ensuring consistent behavior on virtual machines, physical servers, and personal laptops.

Resource Utilization

Containers can be launched without booting an entire operating system, thus reducing resource consumption. We can operate efficiently using fewer resources and minimize our expenditure associated with cloud services or data center operations.

Isolation

By running containers on a single server, each container is isolated from all others thereby ensuring any issue in one specific container does not affect any other container with the same application being run in it.

Agility

Starts, stops, removals—everything happens swiftly because containers are lightweight and self-contained. Due to their quick startup and shutdown times, they are suitable for continuous integration and deployment (CI/CD) pipelines. Fast startup and shutdown times of the containers as compared to virtual machines contribute to faster development and deployment workflows that are more streamlined.

Easy to Scale

Horizontal scaling of containers becomes much easier by running multiple identical application instances. For instance, Kubernetes is a container orchestration tool that can automatically scale containers offering an advanced approach to containerized applications.

Improved Productivity

Often developers say "It works on my machine" meaning their code runs well without any issues in their setup. However, it often fails to work properly in the production environment as per the expectations. Containers solve this problem by providing predictable environments for them, so there is no need to bother about such compatibility problems.

Cloud Support

Major cloud platforms such as Amazon Web Services, Azure, and Google Cloud Platform have embraced containers. In other words, these platforms have adopted container-based services. This is made possible by containers being packaged in a standard format such as the Open Container Initiative (OCI) that enables them to run without any deviation on several cloud platforms. Hence, we can be assured that our application will run in the same way regardless of which cloud environment it runs on.

The following diagram demonstrates some important aspects of containers like their isolation, self-containment, and lightweight design. It also emphasizes its portability meaning that your app could function with flexibility over different clouds.

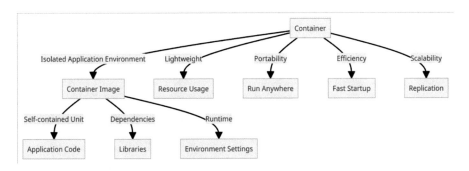

Figure 1-3. *Illustrating essential container attributes*

Container vs. Virtual Machine

You might be wondering whether we should consider containerizing our applications given the fact that VMs are considered the foundation of cloud computing. Some top cloud providers still have services that let you run your application on VMs. Before cloud computing was born, VMs were used for enterprise organizations' mission-critical workloads, and they remain cost-effective and time-saving for business applications.

Furthermore, containers and VMs help efficiently use computer resources but differ in some respects. Let's take a moment to compare the differences between containers and virtual machines.

Table 1-1. *Containers vs. virtual machines*

Criteria	Container	Virtual Machine
Definition	Containers encapsulate an application, its dependencies, libraries, binaries, and configuration files into a single package.	A virtual machine emulates a guest OS and abstracts the physical host machine it is running on.
OS Architecture	Containers do not run full-blown operation systems but share an operating system kernel.	VMs allow us to run multiple full-blown guest operating systems on a host server and improve resource utilization.
Size	Containers are lightweight, containing only the required dependencies to run our applications.	VMs contain an entire guest operating system, so their size is typically large(i.e., in a few GB).
Startup Time	Containers startup time is less (i.e., typically in milliseconds).	VM's startup time is generally in minutes because of its large size.
Runtime Environment	Containers provide a predictable runtime environment.	With VMs, we must spend time and effort to ensure that environments are consistent.
Maintenance	Easy to maintain and upgrade. We can throw away the old container and spin up a new one.	Maintaining and upgrading VMs is cumbersome.

To sum up, containers are maturing and gaining popularity, offering advantages like portability, better resource utilization, isolation, agility, easy scalability, improved productivity, and cloud support. They are suitable for CI/CD pipelines and compatible with multiple operating systems. Comparatively, VMs are efficient for business applications but are larger, take more time to start up, and require more effort to ensure compatibility.

Rise of Docker

Since its introduction in March 2013, Docker has emerged as the undeniable standard for containerizing application workloads. According to the 2024 Stack Overflow developer survey, Docker continues to be at the top of the list among professional developers in the most popular tool category.

Now, let's delve into the factors that have captivated developers and contributed to their fondness for Docker.

Key Reasons for Docker's Popularity

Docker has gained popularity due to several key features and benefits:

- **Cost savings:** Docker is the best choice because it allows us to exploit our existing infrastructure to the fullest. On account of this, Docker containers utilize fewer hardware resources compared to VMs; hence, it becomes a very economical solution. By deploying Docker containers, we can achieve great ROI due to efficient resource utilization.

- **Security:** Applications are well segregated and isolated with Docker which makes it an excellent choice for enterprise settings. It is within this context that Docker's ability to do so has made it the most suitable for use in an enterprise setup. For example, there is a tool called Docker Scout from Docker that inspects image contents and provides a detailed report highlighting packages and vulnerabilities identified. Another thing is that it gives recommendations on how to solve issues detected during image analysis.

- **Easier development:** With the use of Docker, the "It works on my machine" problem can be eliminated since it ensures a consistent environment during all stages of the software development life cycle from local setups right through to production environments. This consistent environment helps developers significantly increase productivity by allowing them not to worry about infrastructure compatibility when writing codes. Furthermore, Docker images are versioned, so it is easy to roll back on previous image versions in case of problems, therefore adding an extra layer of flexibility and stability to the development process.

- **Integration with existing tools:** Docker comes with direct support in several IDEs that are very widely used. This eases container-based application development and management in the inner development loop of the application. Docker's inherent features and support from orchestration tools like Kubernetes make them efficient and resilient in production environments. Besides, Docker easily integrates into GitHub Actions— the widely used CI/CD platform—so that you can automate your pipeline for building, testing, and deploying container applications. Docker has many GitHub Actions available in the market—official, user-contributed—that provide building, annotating, and pushing of images with easy-to-use, reusable components from within our workflows.

- **Microservices architecture:** The rise of microservices architecture demanded a solution to manage the complexity of deploying and scaling multiple services independently. Docker's lightweight and modular nature makes it an excellent candidate for decomposing monolithic applications into microservices. Running stateless Microservices as containers is thus a logical choice. Thus, with this approach, deployments are simple, and scaling is facilitated, by exploiting existing hardware resources optimally. Each microservice can be put inside its container that could be developed, scaled up or down, and deployed autonomously. Airbnb, Netflix, and Paypal have all adopted Docker as a technology for building scalable fault-tolerant architectures of microservices.

- **Hybrid and multi-cloud deployments:** More enterprises are embracing multi-cloud environments to avoid vendor lock-ins and global outages by depending on a single cloud provider. Having said that, each cloud provider comes with different configurations, policies, and tools for management, which makes the deployment of applications complex. Docker's portability allows organizations to deploy applications in a consistent way for both hybrid and multi-cloud setups. We can build applications once and run anywhere using Docker containers, allowing seamless migration and deployment across diverse cloud providers or on-premises infrastructure. For example, a running container in AWS EC2 can easily be moved to an environment within the Google Cloud Platform without change or loss of anything. This is the flexibility that can lower the risk of vendor lock-in and allows businesses to choose the infrastructure that businesses would prefer to use most.

- **Versatility for various scenarios:** Docker is extremely flexible and can be used in a multitude of use cases. In an enterprise setting, when multiple tools and technologies are in use across the team, creating a consistent development environment becomes challenging. This is achievable with Docker, which gives the ability to standardize environments and set them up consistently. We can define infrastructure specifications within a Dockerfile and commit to a code repository. Developers can then effortlessly create their development environments using these specifications. We often rely on third-party tools like PostgreSQL or Nginx in application development. Leveraging container images of these third-party applications simplifies their execution, as all the necessary dependencies are encapsulated within the container. That means minimal manual configuration is required and that one does not have to be wasting a lot of time looking through documentation. This time-saving convenience applies to various tools, including databases and web servers, as container images are frequently available.

Summary

In conclusion, Docker has become the standard for containerizing application workloads due to its efficient utilization of resources, provides segregation and isolation for enterprise environments, ensures a consistent development environment, integrates with numerous developer tools, facilitates deployment of microservices-based architectures, and can be deployed consistently across hybrid and multi-cloud environments.

CHAPTER 2

Docker High-Level Overview

Learn about docker, its architecture, its limitations, and how docker works.

Docker is an open source container management tool, developed by Solomon Hykes, and it has grown to become the most used standard in containerizing application workloads within the last decade since its inception in March 2013. Indeed, Docker changed how we package and deploy applications at scale according to its "build once, run anywhere" principle.

Docker provides a platform for effectively developing, distributing, and running applications as containers. It falls under the category of Platform as a Service within cloud computing.

Docker's Basic Principle

Java popularized the slogan "Write Once, Run Anywhere(WORA)" in software development. That means once written, Java applications can run on any device or platform with a compatible JVM. Docker has taken this one step further: ensuring that the application and all its runtime environment are packaged, distributed, and run uniformly.

© Ashish Choudhary 2025
A. Choudhary, *When Docker Meets Java*, https://doi.org/10.1007/979-8-8688-1300-9_2

Let us now talk about the underlying principle behind how Docker works: Build Once, Run Anywhere(BORA). Consider this: two developers are working on the same application, and they want to run the application on their local machines to speed up the development process. Developer A finally got the application running on their workstation and shared the steps they took with Developer B. When Developer B followed these steps, they couldn't get the application up and running easily.

Why did developer B encounter difficulties when trying to run the application?

Well, there could be multiple answers to this but it could be possible that Developer A unintentionally omitted crucial instructions, such as environment variables to run the application.

Remember: This issue is all too common among developers, leading to frustrating situations where some may assert that "it works on my machine." At the same time, it fails to function on other setups.

This is precisely where Docker shines, assuring that if an application is built using Docker, it will exhibit consistent behavior regardless of the environment—whether it be development, staging, or production. Docker eliminates the discrepancies caused by environment-specific variations, offering a reliable and consistent application execution experience.

Docker Is Not!!!

We know about the features offered by Docker, but it's essential to understand its limitations.

- **Docker is not a virtualization technology:**
  Virtualization technology, like VMware or Hyper-V, creates entire virtual machines with their operating systems, simulating hardware resources. On the other hand, Docker leverages the underlying host's OS and uses containerization, a form of OS-level virtualization. Docker containers share the same OS kernel and isolate

the application processes from each other. It does not emulate hardware or run full-blown guest operating systems.

- **Docker is not a container orchestrator:** Docker, in its core form, is a platform to develop, ship, and run applications inside containers. While Docker provides a simple orchestration solution called Docker Swarm, Docker is not an orchestrator. Tools like Kubernetes, Amazon ECS, or Apache Mesos are dedicated container orchestrators designed to manage, scale, and maintain containerized applications across multiple machines.

- **Docker is not a virtual machine (VM) or a "lightweight VM":** As mentioned earlier, virtual machines emulate hardware resources and run whole operating systems. VMs have their kernel, binaries, and libraries. On the other hand, Docker containers share the host's kernel and encapsulate only the application and its direct dependencies. Containers are significantly more lightweight than VMs, but it would be a misnomer to call them "lightweight VMs" as they operate at a different layer of abstraction.

- **Docker is not the exclusive method for containerizing applications:** While Docker popularized container technology and made it more accessible, it's not the sole method for containerization. Other tools and platforms, like Podman, containerd, and rkt (Rocket), also provide ways to create and manage containers. These might have specific features or design philosophies that distinguish them from Docker, but they serve the same fundamental purpose of containerizing applications.

- **Docker is not a container as a service (CaaS) platform:** CaaS platforms provide container orchestration, management, scaling, and operational features as a service, often in cloud environments. Examples include Google Kubernetes Engine (GKE), Amazon ECS, and Azure Kubernetes Service (AKS). At its core, Docker is a tool designed for the creation and execution of containers. While Docker, Inc. has offered products and services around Docker (e.g., Docker Hub, Docker Enterprise), Docker itself, as a technology, isn't a CaaS solution. It can be part of a CaaS offering but isn't one by itself.

How Does Docker Work?

Docker operates on a client/server architecture, with Docker Engine as the system's central component. Docker Engine consists of the Docker daemon, a REST API, and a command-line interface (CLI). The Docker CLI communicates with the REST API exposed by the Docker daemon. When Docker commands are issued from the CLI, they are received by the Docker daemon, which then executes those commands.

Docker's client-server architecture relies on a main component known as Docker Engine. Docker Engine comprises the Docker daemon, a REST API, and a CLI. The Docker CLI communicates with the REST API exposed by the Docker Daemon. So, when Docker commands are issued from the CLI, they are received by the Docker Daemon, which then executes those commands.

Key Docker Commands

To illustrate, here are the commands in the sequence typically used to create an image:

1. `docker build`: Docker daemon is responsible for building our image.

2. `docker tag`: The image is tagged to a specific version.

3. `docker push`: Finally, the image is pushed to a remote Docker Hub registry.

Another application might want to use our image to run the following commands. Here, all the action is done by the Docker daemon process itself.

1. `docker pull`: Docker first needs the image locally to run our containers. If the image is not found locally, it will get it from the image registry.

2. `docker run`: Once the image is available, we can use this command to start and run the application inside a container.

The Docker CLI executes all the commands we discussed, while the Docker daemon performs the corresponding actions.

The following diagram visually represents the interaction between the Docker CLI, Docker Daemon, Docker REST API, Docker Image Registry, and Docker Containers, providing an overview of the Docker client/server architecture and the flow of commands and data between the components.

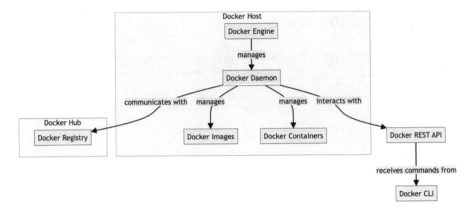

Figure 2-1. *Docker architecture*

Here's what each part represents:

- **Docker engine**: This is the core part of Docker, including the runtime and daemon process. It's the layer on which Docker runs and manages various Docker components.

- **Docker daemon (Dockerd)**: This is a persistent background service that manages Docker images, containers, networks, and volumes. It's the part that does the heavy lifting in the Docker architecture.

- **Docker REST api**: The Docker daemon exposes a REST API used by the Docker Client to communicate with the daemon. It allows users or other tools to interact programmatically with the Docker daemon.

- **Docker cli**: This command-line interface allows users to interact with Docker using commands. When we type a command into the Docker CLI, it sends these commands to the Docker daemon via the Docker REST API.

- **Docker images**: These are read-only templates with instructions for creating Docker containers. Images define the container environment and the application running within the container.

- **Docker containers**: Containers are instances of Docker images executed by the Docker daemon. They isolate applications from the underlying system and each other.

- **Docker registry**: This storage and content delivery system holds named Docker images in different tagged versions. Users interact with a registry by using Docker push and pull commands. Docker Hub is a public instance of a Docker registry that Docker, Inc. operates.

Here's the interaction flow in the Docker architecture as per the diagram:

1. The **Docker CLI** sends a command to the **Docker daemon** via the **Docker REST API**.

2. The **Docker daemon** then communicates with the **Docker Registry** to pull or push images as requested or manages **Docker Images** and **Docker Containers** locally.

3. All these operations are under the umbrella of the **Docker Engine**, which facilitates these components working together seamlessly.

Understanding Docker Desktop

Docker Desktop for macOS and Windows is the fastest, no-clutter way to containerize applications. When Docker came initially, it was targeted for Linux, and there was no official support for other systems like Windows and macOS. After realizing this limitation and huge drawback in their design, the Docker Team decided in something great—the official port to these systems—called Docker Desktop.

According to the official documentation:

Docker Desktop is an application for macOS and Windows machines that is used to build and share containerized applications and microservices.

When drawing analogies, one might think of Docker Desktop as an IDE for containers. Since Windows and macOS do not natively support containers, Docker Desktop compensates by using its light VM. On Windows, it uses Hyper-V or WSL2 (since the former is preferred), and on macOS, it uses Hyperkit. Docker Desktop has a helpful GUI that controls these VM resources.

The advantage of Docker Desktop lies in its streamlined installation process, as it offers a single package for Mac and Windows users. This package includes essential components to utilize Docker effectively.

A typical Docker Desktop installation encompasses the following components:

- Docker Engine
- Docker CLI
- Docker Compose
- Kubernetes
- Content Trust
- Credential Helper

Here's a simplified diagram illustrating the components of Docker Desktop:

> The following diagram provides a high-level overview of how the different components of a Docker Desktop environment work together to enable containerization and management of applications.

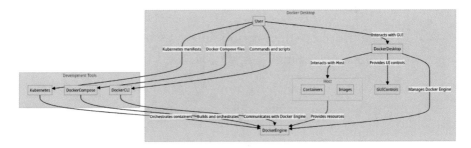

Figure 2-2. *Docker Desktop components*

- The central part of the diagram is Docker Desktop itself, which works directly as the user interface. Users can interact with the Docker Desktop through Kubernetes manifests, Docker Compose files, commands, and scripts.

- Then, the Docker Desktop interacts with the Host that holds the containers and images, which the Docker Engine is responsible for. The core element of Docker is the Docker Engine, which is responsible for orchestrating the containers and providing the necessary resources.

- This diagram further shows several Development Tools that are part of Docker Desktop, including Kubernetes, DockerCompose, and DockerCLI. These tools blend in with the Docker Desktop for additional functionalities and abilities.

Now, let's explore some of the critical features Docker Desktop provides.

Docker Desktop Features

Here are some key features of Docker Desktop:

- Simplified containerization and sharing of applications

- Ability to scan images for potential vulnerabilities

- User-friendly interface for managing Docker components

- Docker Desktop supports multiple system architectures, including Apple M1, ARM, and Windows

- Introduction of Dev Environments for creating consistent and reproducible development environments

- Built-in support for Kubernetes, enabling the creation of functional single-node Kubernetes clusters using Docker Desktop

- Extensibility through third-party tools powered by Docker extensions

- Native support for running Linux on Windows using WSL2

Docker Desktop in Action

Docker Desktop enhances the functionality of the underlying open source Docker components by offering user-friendly maintenance, monitoring, and upgrade features. It delivers a uniform user experience across various operating systems. With Docker Desktop, team collaboration is streamlined through Docker Dev Environments, enabling one-click sharing via Git or Docker Hub. It boasts a straightforward graphical interface for common tasks such as:

- Initiating a container

  You can start a new container with Docker Desktop that is based on a Docker image of your choice.

  You can choose the image and then optionally set settings for port mapping, environment variables, and volumes. It then launches the container in one click.

  This simplifies the process of spinning up new containerized applications, so users new to Docker can start easily.

- Pausing and restarting a container

  Docker Desktop offers a graphical user interface to pause and resume running containers.

  Pausing a container suspends its execution, allowing you to temporarily stop the container's activity without losing its state.

  Restarting the paused container resumes its operation from the point where it was paused.

  This feature is useful for temporarily suspending a container's activities, for example, during maintenance or debugging.

- Stopping a container

  The Docker Desktop interface allows you to easily stop running containers.

  It stops a container gently and closes the application or process running inside the container.

  This is useful if you have to stop a container and release the resources that container was using.

- Configuring a local Kubernetes cluster

  Docker Desktop provides built-in functionality
  to create and manage a local Kubernetes cluster.
  The user can enable and configure a single-node
  Kubernetes cluster directly from the Docker Desktop
  interface.

  This helps developers test and develop applications
  using Kubernetes without an additional separate
  Kubernetes setup.

- Managing volumes

  Docker desktop allows a developer to manage the
  volumes by creating, inspecting, and mounting a
  volume right from the UI of the Docker desktop.

This therefore simplifies the process of managing persistent storage for
your containerized applications and will thus ensure that no data is lost
when the containers are stopped or removed.

To show the capabilities of the docker desktop, let's try to run a
pre-built image from Dockerhub.

- Look for the Docker Desktop icon on our Desktop.
  Double-click the Docker Desktop icon to launch the
  application.

- To locate images, click the search bar at the top or use
  the shortcut ⌘ + K. To find the specific image used in
  this guide, search for "welcome-to-docker".

- Choose **Run**.

- Upon the display of **Optional settings**, enter the Host port number 8090, and then click **Run**. This will map the internal port of the container to the host port specified and allow access to the application running in the container from the host machine.

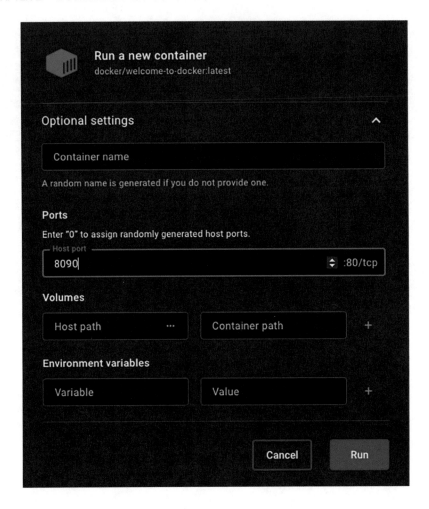

- Go to the Containers tab in Docker Desktop to view the container.

- Click the link given under Port(s).

- We should see the following output.

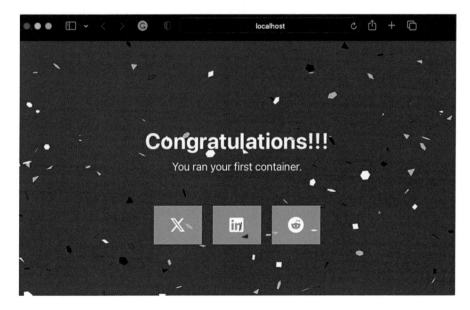

- We also have the option to stop the container.

- We have multiple options to manage containers, that is, restart/pause.

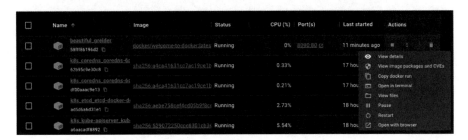

To conclude, Docker Desktop simplifies containerizing applications and microservices for macOS and Windows users. It provides a graphical interface for managing VM resources and offers streamlined installation. Features include simplified containerization and sharing, image scanning, support for multiple system architectures, Dev Environments, and built-in support for Kubernetes.

Key Docker Concepts

Let's understand Docker by drawing parallels with familiar Java principles. In the next sections, let's look at constituents and associated terminologies by relating them to the already familiar landscape of Java development.

Dockerfile

Docker relies on a text document named Dockerfile when constructing a container image. This file encompasses a series of instructions that define the construction of the Docker image. In Java terms, we can say that Dockerfile is akin to a Java class definition. It contains instructions on how to build a Docker image. Just as a Java class specifies how to create objects, a Dockerfile outlines the steps to construct a Docker image.

For a basic Java/Spring Boot application, the Dockerfile typically includes the following set of instructions.

```
FROM openjdk:17
COPY target/*.jar app.jar
ENTRYPOINT ["java","-jar","/app.jar"]
```

The FROM instruction specifies the base image that serves as the foundation for our application.

The COPY instruction copies the locally built .jar file generated by the chosen build tool, such as Maven, Ant, or Gradle, into our container image.

As for the ENTRYPOINT instruction, it designates the default executable command for our container upon startup. In this example, we aim to run the .jar file using the java -jar command.

Docker Image

Similar to how a JAR file packages a Java application and its dependencies, a Docker image encapsulates an application, including its runtime, libraries, and dependencies. Both serve as self-contained units ready for deployment. Also, just as JAR files can be distributed and shared easily, Docker images can be effortlessly distributed and shared, allowing users to push and pull from Docker registries like Docker Hub and facilitating the seamless sharing and distribution of applications.

Docker CLI

The Docker CLI (Command-Line Interface) is the primary means of interacting with Docker. Commands issued from the CLI are transmitted to the Docker daemon using these communication channels. In Java, JShell allows developers to enter and execute Java code snippets interactively, and the Docker CLI enables developers to execute commands for managing Docker components.

Docker Container

A Docker container is like an instance of a Java class. It's a runnable environment created from a Docker image, similar to how objects are created from a class in Java. Each container is isolated and runs its application or service.

Docker Daemon

Docker daemon acts as the Docker core component, like the central nervous system. It runs as a background service in the host system and is responsible for executing the commands—like `docker build`, `docker pull`, and `docker run`—issued through the Docker CLI. It's comparable to a JVM running in the background. It is responsible for running and managing Docker containers, similar to the way in which the JVM manages the execution of Java applications.

Docker Hub

Docker Hub is the image repository where we can store, share, and manage container images. Think of a Docker Hub as a central repository for storing Docker images, similar to how Maven Central Repository stores Java libraries. Docker Hub, for example, is like a Maven repository for Docker images.

Docker Compose

As application developers, in most cases we would be dealing with applications comprising several components, such as a front-end API and a back-end API. Say, for example, that the application requires extra features such as an Nginx web server and a database that the back-end API uses to serve data back to the front-end API. Running and managing these varied components as separate containers can get very tricky, with several Docker commands needed to assure the running of the entire application cohesively. To solve this problem, in comes Docker Compose. Docker Compose is a tool for running multiple containers, so they all work together in harmony. This is done through the definition of services using a docker-compose.yml file, outlining the configuration and dependencies of various containers needed for an application. It will be possible to efficiently streamline running and management of the whole application stack using Docker Compose.

It's much more of a Java build tool, such as Maven or Gradle. In Maven, for example, a configuration file named `pom.xml` holds the configuration of a project and its dependencies; similarly to Docker, in Docker, there is also one configuration file, usually `docker-compose.yml`, that defines multicontainer Docker applications.

A Sample `docker-compose.yml` file.

```
version: '3'
services:
  app:
    build: .
    image: my-java-app
    ports:
      - "8080:8080"
    environment:
      - SPRING_PROFILES_ACTIVE=prod
```

Here is an image illustrating Docker concepts.

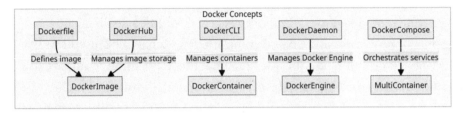

Figure 2-3. *Docker concepts and their relationships*

In other words, what Docker knowledge for Java developers can be easier if one finds a way to compare it to the most familiar principles of Java. So, Dockerfile is much like a definition of a Java class with instructions regarding how to build a Docker image. A Docker image does for an application, runtime libraries, and dependencies what a JAR file does. The Docker CLI is the primary interface to interact with Docker, and Docker daemon acts as its central nervous system. Docker Hub is for image storage, sharing, and management. Docker Compose enables orchestrating several containers working together seamlessly, like Java build tools, for configuration and dependency management across projects.

Summary

The chapter introduces Docker as an open source container management tool that has revolutionized the way applications are packaged and deployed. It explains Docker's core principle of "Build Once, Run Anywhere" (BORA), which ensures consistent application behavior across different environments, in contrast to the common "It works on my machine" problem.

Then the chapter clarifies what Docker is not—a virtualization technology, or a container orchestrator, or a virtual machine, or the only method for containerizing applications. These descriptions help differentiate Docker from related but quite different concepts.

Then, it goes into how Docker works with its client-server architecture around the Docker Engine. It explains how the Docker CLI communicates with the Docker daemon to run commands like build, tag, push, pull, and run.

In the section about Docker Desktop, it explains how GUI application meant to make life easier using Docker on macOS and Windows: simplified containerization, scanning images, multicontainer support for numerous system architectures, and integration into tools such as Kubernetes.

The last part of the chapter introduces key Docker concepts and draws comparisons with well-known Java development principles. It explains how a Docker file is similar to the definition of a Java class, an image in Docker is akin to a JAR file, the CLI in Docker is similar to JShell, a container in Docker is similar to a Java object, a daemon in Docker is equivalent to a JVM, a Docker Hub is similar to Maven Central, and Compose in Docker is like the build tools in Java, for instance, Maven or Gradle.

CHAPTER 3

Up and Running with Docker

Among the many tools available for application packaging and deployment, Docker is one of the most important in containerization. One of the key elements in this process is the Dockerfile, which represents a blueprint of the configuration, dependencies, and steps followed to build a Docker image. It consists of several instructions that allow us to build containers using the `docker build` command.

Creating a Dockerfile

To commence, let's start by creating an empty Dockerfile. Remember to name it with a capital "D," that is, Dockerfile, without any file extension. By default, the docker build command looks for a file named "Dockerfile" (with a capital "D") in the specified context.

If we name it `dockerfile` or anything else, we will need to specify the Docker build file using the `-f` or `--file` flag during the build process.

Step 1: Create a new directory on the terminal by running the command `mkdir docker`. Navigate to the directory using the command `cd docker`.

Step 2: Now run `touch Dockerfile`, creating an empty Dockerfile for us.

© Ashish Choudhary 2025
A. Choudhary, *When Docker Meets Java*, https://doi.org/10.1007/979-8-8688-1300-9_3

Step 3: Run the vi Dockerfile command and paste the following content. To save the change, press Esc to exit insert mode, then type :wq, and press Enter.

```
FROM alpine:latest
RUN apk --no-cache add git
CMD git --version
```

- We use the alpine base OS image in the FROM command. It is a minimal, simple, secure image based on Alpine Linux. It is only 5 MB in size.

- In the RUN command, we use the apk; the package manager will install Git inside the container image. This command is only executed when we build the container image.

- In the CMD command, we use the git --version command executed when we run the container image.

Step 4: Build the image by executing the docker build . command with the Dockerfile.

The . (dot) represents the build context. By using . (dot) as the build context, we are instructing Docker to look for the Dockerfile and associated files in the current directory and use them to build the Docker image.

Step 5: Run the docker image ls(to list down images) command and note down IMAGE ID of the container image.

Step 6: Execute the docker run --rm -it IMAGE ID command. Ensure that we paste the previously noted IMAGE ID. This command will display the git version as the output when we run the container image.

The -it flags ensure an interactive session with the container, allowing us to see and interact with the output if necessary. The -rm flag automatically removes the container when it exits. This helps clean the system after the container is executed.

The image below demonstrates the process by which a Dockerfile generates a container.

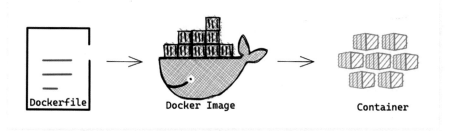

Figure 3-1. *Docker image creation flow*

To summarize, we will have a handwritten Dockerfile, which we will use to build the Docker Image. Later on, we will use that image to run a container.

Let's talk about commands that we can use while writing a Dockerfile.

Dockerfile Commands and Their Usage

Table 3-1. *Common Dockerfile commands*

Command	Usage	Example
ENV	Sets environment variables inside the image	`ENV APP_HOME=/usr/src/app`
Label	Use to specify metadata for image, i.e., email id of the maintainer, etc.	`LABEL maintainer="your-email@example.com"`
EXPOSE	Port through which we can access our application	`EXPOSE 8080`
CMD	Use to pass arguments to **ENTRYPOINT**. If **ENTRYPOINT** is not set, then the command in **CMD** gets executed	`CMD ["app.jar"]`
ENTRYPOINT	Specify commands that get executed when we start the container	`ENTRYPOINT ["java", "-jar"]`
WORKDIR	Current working directory	`WORKDIR $APP_HOME`
RUN	To install packages required for our application	`RUN apt-get update && apt-get install -y openjdk-11-jre`
ADD	Same as **COPY** but can also download and copy files from remote URLs. It can also decompress compressed files to the destination	`ADD https://example.com/external-app.jar $APP_HOME/app.jar`
COPY	As the name suggests, it copies over files and directories from a source to a destination location	`COPY ./local-app-config $APP_HOME/config`
FROM	Foundation layer upon which all other layers are built	`FROM ubuntu:latest`

Exploring Facts About Dockerfiles

Dockerfiles are not executable code: A Dockerfile represents commands for image execution at build time. This isn't directly executable like it was a program.

```
# Dockerfile
FROM openjdk:17-jdk
WORKDIR /app
COPY target/myapp.jar /app
CMD ["java", "-jar", "myapp.jar"]
```

Build and run:

```
docker build -t my-java-app .
docker run my-java-app
```

Layer caching: Docker uses a layered file system for its images, where instructions in a Dockerfile are cached as layers to be used in accelerating subsequent builds.

```
FROM openjdk:17-jdk
WORKDIR /app
COPY pom.xml /app  # Cached if pom.xml doesn't change
RUN mvn dependency:go-offline  # Dependencies are cached
COPY src /app/src
RUN mvn package  # Rebuilds only if src changes
```

Order matters: Since the layers are cached, the order in which you have the instructions in a Dockerfile is significant. If you change an instruction, all future layers become invalid and need to be rebuilt.

```
# Inefficient
FROM openjdk:17-jdk
WORKDIR /app
```

```
COPY src /app/src
COPY pom.xml /app
RUN mvn package  # Rebuilds everything if pom.xml changes
# Efficient
FROM openjdk:17-jdk
WORKDIR /app
COPY pom.xml /app
RUN mvn dependency:go-offline  # Cache dependencies
COPY src /app/src
RUN mvn package
```

Multiple base images: Even though one can use only the FROM instruction with a Dockerfile, we can do that by using multi-stage builds, making it possible to bring artifacts from different bases into one image.

```
# Stage 1: Build
FROM maven:3.8-openjdk-17 as builder
WORKDIR /app
COPY . .
RUN mvn clean package -DskipTests
# Stage 2: Minimal runtime
FROM openjdk:17-jre
WORKDIR /app
COPY --from=builder /app/target/myapp.jar /app
CMD ["java", "-jar", "myapp.jar"]
```

Dangling images: Images created with a tag that is later replaced by another image become "dangling images," consuming space until they are pruned.

```
$docker image prune  # Remove dangling images
```

Image labeling: With Docker, it is possible to add metadata to images using labels, and the kind of information that one can provide includes version, maintainer, or arbitrary information.

```
FROM openjdk:17-jdk
LABEL maintainer="you@example.com"
LABEL version="1.0.0"
LABEL description="Java Spring Boot application"
```

Escape characters: Dockerfile supports backslashes (\) for escaping, but beware of inconsistencies with Windows paths; prefer double backslashes (\\) or forward slashes.

```
# Use forward slashes or double backslashes for Windows
COPY config/app-config.json /app/config/
```

Size optimization: Be wary of your use of the instruction COPY, as it may inflate your images. Minimize this by using wildcards, so you only copy necessary files.

```
# Avoid copying unnecessary files
COPY target/*.jar /app/
```

Security concerns: Don't hardcode secrets in the Dockerfile. Pass sensitive data securely through the build arguments or environment variables.

```
FROM openjdk:17-jdk
ARG API_KEY
ENV API_KEY=${API_KEY}
CMD ["java", "-jar", "myapp.jar"]
```

Pass secrets securely during build:

```
docker build --build-arg API_KEY=mysecretkey -t my-java-app .
```

Building and Tagging a Docker Image

In this section, you will learn how to build an image using Dockerfile. Explore different strategies to tag an image.

The `docker build` command allows us to construct an image using the Dockerfile and a context. The context denotes a collection of files accessible via a specific path or URL. It's important to note that the build context operates recursively, meaning files in subdirectories are also included in the process. Consequently, we should execute the docker build command from a directory containing only the Dockerfile.

Alternatively, we can employ a `.dockerignore` file to specify which files we want to exclude from the docker build process.

The `docker build` command supports various flags, offering additional options and functionalities during the image construction.

Example

Let's follow a step-by-step coding example to demonstrate building, tagging, and pushing a Docker image for a simple Java application to DockerHub.

Step 1. Directory setup: Assume we have a basic Java application with the following file structure:

```
my-java-app/
    ├── src/
    │   └── Main.java
    └── Dockerfile
```

Step 2. Create the java application: Let's create a simple Java application in the Main.java file:

```
public class Main {
    public static void main(String[] args) {
        System.out.println("Hello,Docker!");
    }
}
```

Step 3. Create the dockerfile: Next, we need to create a Dockerfile to define the Docker image:

```
FROM eclipse-temurin:17-jdk-jammy
COPY ./src /app
WORKDIR /app
RUN javac Main.java
CMD ["java","Main"]
```

This Dockerfile uses the official OpenJDK 17 image as the base, copies the Main.java file into the image, compiles it, and finally sets the command to run the compiled Java application.

Step 4. Build the docker image: Open the terminal or command prompt, and ensure we are inside the directory having Dockerfile on the terminal and type the following command.

```
$ docker build -t my-java-app:1.0 .
```

This command will build the Docker image with the tag (by using the -t flag) my-java-app:1.0 as the build context. Setting the image name and tag while building our image is good practice. The . (dot) at the end of the command indicates to Docker that Dockerfile is present in the current working directory.

Step 5. Verify the built docker image: To verify that the Docker image was built successfully, run the following command:

```
$ docker images
```

We should see the my-java-app image with the 1.0 tag listed among our local Docker images.

Step 6. Tag the docker image for dockerhub: Now, we'll tag the Docker image to prepare it for pushing to DockerHub:

```
$ docker tag my-java-app:1.0 our-dockerhub-username/
my-java-app:1.0
```

Note   Replace our-dockerhub-username with our actual DockerHub username.

Here's a simplified diagram that outlines the Docker image build process:

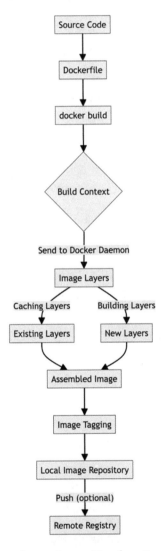

Figure 3-2. *Building and tagging a Docker image*

In this flow:

- The process starts with our source code and a Dockerfile.

- The `docker build` command initiates the build process.

- The build context, which includes our source code and any other files in the directory or specified in the Dockerfile, is sent to the Docker daemon.

- Docker then assembles the image in layers, utilizing the cache to speed up the build process.

- New layers are created as needed based on instructions in the Dockerfile.

- The assembled image is then optionally tagged with a name.

- The final image is stored in our local image repository.

- We can then push the image to a remote registry if desired.

Tagging a Docker Image

Tagging a Docker image is a best practice that brings numerous benefits throughout the software development and deployment life cycle. Image tagging is the process of assigning a meaningful label to an image, which can be used to differentiate its version, purpose, or environment. And here's why it's so important:

Benefits of Image Tagging

1. **Versioning and history**: Tagging can also be used to differentiate the various versions we have of our images. For instance, while updating our application, we can tag images with version numbers like v1.0 and v2.0, or the dates on which they were taken such as 2023-07-17. This helps to maintain a history of changes and provides a way back if needed.

2. **Deployment and rollback**s: If you are deploying an application into various environments— development, testing, and production—you can use tags to ensure that the appropriate image version is used in each environment. If a problem shows up in production, we're able to easily roll back to a previous state with the tagged image.

3. **Collaboration**: Tagging offers one of the most exact reference points for collaboration among developers. It allows team members to use the same tagged image, thereby ensuring consistency across development and testing environments.

4. **Tagging**: Use tagging to promote images across the various stages of the development pipeline. At each stage of the pipeline, from local development, through testing, to production, we can tag an image as it passes, thus keeping a reliable version at each step.

5. **Microservices/distributed systems**: There are times when services could rely on specific versions of other services inside the space of a microservice or distributed system. Tagging, in this regard, becomes really relevant to making sure that services can be found and used at compatible versions of their dependents.

6. **Continuous integration/continuous deployment (CI/CD)**: This automates the pipeline, image creation, and deployment. Tags enable these pipelines to have a way of finding an exact version of an image and then tracking it at every stage throughout the pipeline.

7. **Rollback and recovery**: In case a problem arises after deploying a new application version, with tagged images, we can quickly roll back to the previous version, thus reducing downtime and possible impacts.

8. **Documentation**: Tagging is a way of documenting. An image tag is supposed to present useful information on the purpose and use of the image, the version, or any other important thing.

9. **Testing and quality assurance**: Tagged images ensure that the tested version remains consistent with what will be deployed.

10. **Image pruning**: As we build and tag new iterations of our images, we can delete the older images with out-of-date tags to save on storage space.

Image Tagging Strategies

Let's understand some advanced image tagging strategies past just version numbers, so they offer clarity, traceability, and most importantly, consistency. It is by having consistent and meaningful tag methods that Docker images become easily managed—hence making it easy for you to identify and deploy the preferred image versions with ease.

1. **Semantic versioning**: Tagging with semantic versioning is a common strategy to indicate the significance of an image. For example, if this image is meant for a specific release of our application:

   ```
   $ docker build -t my-java-app:1.0.0 .
   ```

2. **Using the git commit hash**: Tag images based on respective git commit hash, so they can be traced back to specific versions of code. This is very useful in:

   ```
   $ docker build -t my-java-app .
   ```

3. **Environment-specific tags**: In case we are building images for various environments, for example, development, testing, and production, we can use environment-specific tags as follows:

   ```
   $ docker build -t my-java-app .
   $ docker build -t my-java-app .
   $ docker build -t my-java-app .
   ```

4. **Date-based tags**: Tagging the build date of an image helps to trace the creation date of an image:

   ```
   $ docker build -t my-java-app:2023-08-17 .
   ```

5. **Latest tag**: Using the `latest` tag for the latest build is a convenience, but not the best practice in a production environment due to the ambiguity it has:

```
$ docker build -t my-java-app .
```

In conclusion, we can build a Docker image by using the `docker build` command to a Dockerfile and a context. The context is all the files in a certain path or URL. In this case, the `docker build` command will have numerous flags available to offer extra options. This is crucial in tagging for version control, history tracking, practices in deployment, collaboration, and the ability to promote images between different stages of the development pipeline.

Pushing and Running a Docker Image

In this section, we will learn about container management and discover the art of efficiently pushing Docker images to registries like DockerHub and seamlessly deploying them.

In the world of containerization for deployment, Docker images are pushed to remote container registries. The concept of pushing a Docker image is that we want to upload our locally built Docker image to a remote image registry, that is, Docker Hub or private registry.

The following are some of the highlights of pushing an image to registries like DockerHub with the help of `docker push` command:

1. **Image distribution**: It allows us to push our images to distribute the Docker images in a remote location. They have shared that making images available for others' use, developers, and systems is crucial for collaboration and deployment on heterogeneous environments.

2. **Centralized image storage**: The Docker registries form centralized repositories for the storage and management of Docker images. When we push our images to a registry, there is one source of truth for the images that several teams and projects can access.

3. **Consistent deployments**: Pushing images to a registry will ensure that the same image is present throughout development environments, through testing, and up to production. This greatly minimizes risks that come from a lack of consistency between different versions of the same image.

4. **Share with others**: Should we decide to share our application with colleagues, clients, or the open source community, pushing images to a public registry—such as Docker Hub—allows other people to pull and run our application quickly, without building it on their machine.

5. **Private registries**: Organizations often use private registries for the storage of proprietary or sensitive images. By pushing images to a private registry, access is restricted only to authorized users.

6. **CI/CD pipelines**: Whenever a new image is built, it needs to be pushed to the container registry using the CI/CD. Then the following stages of the pipeline—testing or deployment—will be done using that image.

7. **Version control**: We store a history of versions by pushing different versions of our images with unique tags to the registry. This would enable rolling back to a former version if necessary.

8. **Scalability**: For applications deployed on many nodes, servers, or clusters, putting images into a registry ensures all the instances have the same image, resulting in better consistency of scaling and efficiency.

9. **Saves on deployment time**: If we need to have more than one instance of an application, we can save a lot of time and resources just by pulling the image from the registry instead of having to build them on each instance.

10. **Disaster recovery**: In the case of data loss or system failure, the application images will have been pushed to a registry and can be restored in a short time.

Now, we'll use the docker push command to push Docker image to DockerHub:

```
$ docker push our-dockerhub-username/my-java-app:1.0
```

Here is an image illustrating the sequence of Docker commands.

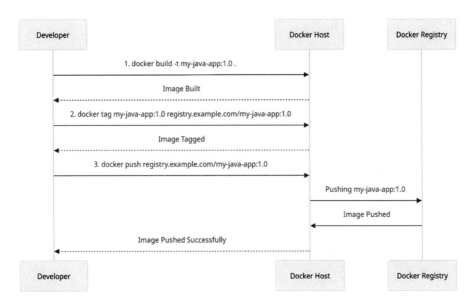

Figure 3-3. *Pushing a Docker image*

Running a Docker Image

Running a Docker image is a straightforward process that allows developers to execute their containerized applications quickly. So we just finished our previous coding example for a simple Java application, by successfully building the image, tagging it, and pushing the Docker image to DockerHub. Now, let's see how we can run that Docker image in the form of a Docker container.

Open your terminal or command prompt and enter the following command to download the Docker image from DockerHub:

```
$ docker pull our-dockerhub-username/my-java-app:1.0
```

Note   Replace our-dockerhub-username with our actual DockerHub username.

With the image successfully pulled, we can now run it as a Docker container:

```
$ docker run our-dockerhub-username/my-java-app:1.0
```

Instantly, we will see the containerized Java application in action, with the console output displaying "Hello, Docker!" as it runs the Java code from within the container. This way, everything related to the application will be isolated from the host system so that dependencies or configurations described by the Docker image are self-sufficient.

Running a Docker image allows developers to quickly test their applications within a controlled environment, without fear of conflicting dependencies or system-specific issues. This all means that development and deployment are simplified with the guarantee of consistent behavior across diverse platforms and environments.

Common Pitfalls

There are several things to watch out for, or common pitfalls when developers are running a Docker image to achieve a smooth and trouble-free experience.

- **Port mapping**: Make sure your port mapping is accurate so we do not run into any inaccessible applications.

- **Volume mounting**: Never forget to mount the volumes that are required to prevent loss of data or unexpected behaviors.

- **Resource constraints**: Define resource constraints, such as for CPU and memory, for prevention from performance erosion or resource contention.

- **Environment variables**: Verify all relevant environment variables to ensure they are appropriately configured and would not cause any errors or unexpected behavior.

- **Sensitive information**: Do not disclose sensitive data, such as passwords or API keys.

- **Host system interference**: Manages the interaction between applications running in containers and on hosts to ensure no unintentional tampering or security weaknesses.

- **Image versioning**: Always use a specific version of a Docker image.

- **Clean Up**: Clean up stopped containers and unused images regularly to free up disk space.

- **Entrypoint and Cmd**: Understand the difference between ENTRYPOINT and CMD in a Dockerfile.

- **Networking**: Make sure the containers that need to talk to each other are networked under the same network.

By going through the Docker documentation, confirming the configuration, and proper testing of the container, one can ensure a reliable and efficient deployment of an application. A correctly configured and thoroughly tested application goes a long way in ensuring that potential issues do not jeopardize the reliability and efficiency of containerized application deployment.

In simple words, to push a Docker image, developers have to use the docker push command to transfer the locally built image to a remote container registry. With only one command, docker run, one can easily run a Docker image. It is easy to run a Docker image, but common pitfalls should be taken care of, like incorrect port mapping or missing volume mounting.

Inspecting and Managing a Docker Image

In this section, you will learn how to debug an issue with a Docker container. Explore different ways to manage a Docker image.

While Docker simplifies the creation and distribution of applications, they have their own set of issues. Therefore, you need to inspect and manage Docker images to ensure that applications are fit, secure, and reliable—just like in traditional software development, due diligence is required. It acts as a safety net against issues possibly escalating to the end users. Ensuring Docker images are free from issues or probable problems is important.

Consider a real-world scenario: A company deployed a containerized web application, but was unknown to them that the base image had a known vulnerability. Attackers can exploit this to their advantage, and this could result in a data breach or service disruption. If appropriate inspection and analysis of the image have been done before deployment, then these risks would be reduced.

Now, let us see how to inspect a Docker image for any underlying issues using a simple Java application.

Step 1. Pull the docker image: The first step is to ensure we have the latest version of the Docker image by pulling it from DockerHub:

```
$ docker pull our-dockerhub-username/my-java-app:1.0
```

Replace *our-dockerhub-username* with our actual DockerHub username and `1.0` with the appropriate version tag.

Step 2. Run the docker container: Run the Docker container from the pulled image to test its functionality:

```
$ docker run our-dockerhub-username/my-java-app:1.0
```

Check the container's console output for any errors or unexpected behavior. If the Java application prints "Hello, Docker!" as expected, it's a positive indication of a functioning image. However, issues may still exist, especially when running more complex applications.

Step 3. Inspect the container's filesystem: To investigate the container's filesystem, we can use Docker's interactive mode:

```
$ docker run -it our-dockerhub-username/my-java-app:1.0 /
bin/bash
```

This command drops us into the container's shell, allowing us to explore its contents interactively. Here, we can verify the presence of all necessary files, libraries, and configurations expected in our Java application.

Step 4. Check for environmental variables: If our Java application relies on environment variables, ensure they are correctly set when running the container. Use the following command to inspect the environment variables:

```
$ docker inspect our-container-id | grep "Environment"
```

Replace *our-container-id* with the container's ID or name. Verify that all required environment variables are present and correctly defined.

Step 5. Verify networking and ports: If our Java application communicates with other services or requires network access, ensure that the necessary ports are correctly mapped:

```
$ docker ps
```

This command will display the ports the container exposes to the host system. Verify that the required ports are correctly mapped and accessible.

Step 6. Analyze docker logs: Review the container's logs to identify any errors or issues:

```
$ docker logs our-container-id
```

Replace *our-container-id* with the container's ID or name. Check for any error messages or stack traces indicating underlying problems.

Docker initiates a process within the container and gathers the output streams from this process as logs. By default, Docker uses the `json-file` driver, which writes these logs in JSON format to a file.

Here is an image illustrating the interaction between the application, the output streams, and Docker.

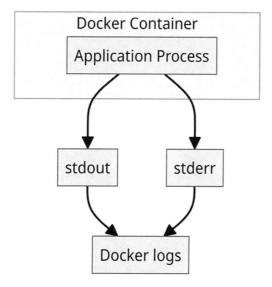

Figure 3-4. *Docker logging flow*

Checking a Docker image for any issues is essential for smooth deployments and reliable applications. Following these steps and using Docker's many tools for inspection, we can reliably identify and fix potential problems in our Dockerized Java application. In this way, the proactive approach of image inspection is going to spare our time and effort in delivering high-quality, containerized applications that work everywhere as expected. Happy Dockerizing!

Managing a Docker Image

Management of Docker images comprises several activities that one needs to do to handle the images efficiently in our containerized applications. Here are a few ways that we can manage Docker images:

- **Search image**: The command `docker search` followed by a keyword shall show the available images in any registry.

- **Delete images**: This is done via the `docker rmi image_name:tag` command. We cannot delete an image if there are running containers based on this image. The -f flag forces removal.

- **Cleanup unused images**: Unused images can accumulate over time. All dangling, or unused, images are removed via `docker image prune`.

- **Image history**: See what makes up an image, that is, layers, and see the commands used to build a given image via `docker history image_name`.

- **Image pruning**: The `docker system prune` removes all unused images, containers, and networks. Note that it removes all unused data.

- **Image scanning**: Docker security scanning is a feature of Docker that enables us to discover vulnerabilities in the components—software packages, libraries, etc.—of our Docker images.

There are several operations that we can perform on Docker images to manage them efficiently. These include searching for available images in a registry by using the `docker search` command, deleting images by using the `docker rmi` command, removing unused images with `docker image` prune, checking an image's history with the `docker history` command, and lastly, `docker system prune` to remove all unused images, containers, and networks. These are tasks that can help manage Docker images effectively and aid the smooth functioning of containerized applications.

Summary

This chapter gives a comprehensive guide to understanding and working with Docker, focusing on Dockerfiles and container management. It introduces Dockerfiles as blueprints for building container images, detailing key commands like FROM, RUN, CMD, COPY, and EXPOSE. Best practices include optimizing image size, managing secrets, and using multi-stage builds.

The chapter explains the image-building process, tagging strategies, and steps for pushing, pulling, and running images. It talks about debugging, image management, and commands to inspect and clean up resources.

The chapter also highlights common mistakes such as wrong port mapping, resource mismanagement, and security oversights and focuses on scanning images and protection of sensitive data.

In the end, the chapter summarizes the benefits of using Docker, such as having consistent environments, simplified distribution, scalability, and resource usage.

## CHAPTER 4

Learning Advanced Docker Concepts

Discover how Docker containers communicate and explore various Docker networking drivers. Learn how to enable data persistence with containers using docker volumes. Know how to create, configure, and manage multicontainer applications with Docker.

Exploring Docker's Networking

Networking is about communication between processes, and Docker's networking functions similarly. Docker networking mainly involves facilitating interaction between Docker containers and the external world through the host machine on which the Docker daemon operates.

Docker supports diverse network types, each tailored for specific usage scenarios. We'll delve into Docker's supported network drivers in general, accompanied by code examples.

Docker's Networking vs. VM Networking

Docker's networking diverges from networking in virtual machines (VMs) or physical machines in several ways:

© Ashish Choudhary 2025
A. Choudhary, *When Docker Meets Java*, https://doi.org/10.1007/979-8-8688-1300-9_4

Here's the information presented in a tabular format.

Feature	VMs	Docker
Networking Configurations	Supports flexible configurations like NAT and host networking.	Primarily uses a bridge network; host networking is mostly supported on Linux.
Network Isolation	Separate networking stack for each VM.	Achieved via a network namespace.
Scale of Networking	Hosts fewer processes per VM, simplifying networking requirements.	Handles numerous containers on a single host, requiring robust networking support.

Types of Docker Network Drivers

Docker simplifies container communication by creating a default bridge network, sparing users from grappling with networking intricacies and allowing them to concentrate on container creation and operation. While this default bridge network suffices in most cases, alternatives exist.

Docker presents three primary network drivers out of the box:

- bridge

- host

- none

However, since these might only suit some context, we'll also delve into user-defined networks like overlay and macvlan. Let's examine each in more detail.

Bridge Driver

This serves as the default driver. When we initiate Docker, a bridge network is established, and all newly launched containers will automatically connect to this default bridge network.

We can employ this when we want isolated containers to communicate internally. Given the segregation of containers, the bridge network effectively resolves port conflicts. It resolves port conflicts by providing each container with its internal IP address within the bridge network's subnet. Containers within the same bridge network can interact, while Docker utilizes iptables on the host machine to restrict access beyond the bridge.

Following is an example describing how the bridge network driver operates:

- Check available networks using the `docker network ls` command.

- Launch two detached busybox (BusyBox a lightweight container provides a single executable file that contains many common Unix utilities, such as `ls`, `cat`, and `echo`, making it ideal for environments where storage and resources are limited) containers, naming them `container1` and `container2`, using the `docker run -dit` command.

    Here, in `-dit` flag d is for detached mode, and `it` ensures that bash or `sh` can be allocated to a pseudo-terminal.

    ```
    docker run -dit --name container1 busybox /bin/sh
    docker run -dit --name container2 busybox /bin/sh
    ```

- Verify that the containers are up and running using the docker ps.

```
$ docker ps
CONTAINER ID    IMAGE       COMMAND      CREATED
STATUS            PORTS      NAMES
8a6464e82c4u    busybox     "/bin/sh"    6 seconds ago
Up 6 seconds              container2
9bea14032749    busybox     "/bin/sh"    28 seconds
ago    Up 28 seconds             container1
```

In Docker, the PORTS section in the output of docker ps is empty when the containers are started with the -d (detached) option and do not explicitly expose or publish any ports.

- Confirm that the containers are connected to the bridge network with the docker network inspect bridge. Note down the IP addresses of both containers.

- Attach to **container1** using docker attach command and attempt to ping the **container2** using its IP address.

```
$ docker attach container1
/ # whoami
root
/ # hostname -i
182.18.0.2
/ # ping 182.18.0.3
PING 182.18.0.3 (182.18.0.3): 56 data bytes
64 bytes from 182.18.0.3: seq=0 ttl=64 time=2.083 ms
64 bytes from 182.18.0.3: seq=1 ttl=64 time=0.144 ms
```

- Please remember that we don't recommend using the bridge driver for production scenarios. It is ideal for single-host setups where all containers run on the same Docker host.

- Communication between containers relies on IP addresses rather than automatic service discovery for translating IP addresses to container names.

- The bridge driver can also permit unrelated containers to communicate, potentially posing a security hazard.

Host Driver

As the name implies, the host driver leverages the host machine's networking. This removes network isolation between the container and the host machine where Docker operates.

```
$docker run --rm -d --network host --name my_nginx nginx
```

--network host: Uses the host network, meaning the container shares the host's network namespace. The container will directly bind to the host's ports without Docker's network isolation.

For example, the official Nginx image listens on port 80 by default; when a container bound to port **80** employs host networking, the container's application is accessible on port 80 via the host's IP address. So in this case, If the host machine's port 80 is not already in use, you can access Nginx at `http://localhost:80/`.

This driver is Linux-specific and isn't available on Docker desktop installations. We can leverage it if we want to depend on the host machine's networking rather than Docker's.

None Driver

This driver avoids attaching containers to any network. Containers remain cut off from the external network and communication with other containers.

This driver is helpful when we need to deactivate networking on a container.

Overlay and macvlan Drivers

The overlay driver supports multi-host communication, often used in environments like Docker Swarm or Kubernetes. It allows containers across hosts to interact without intricate setups. It's like a virtualized distributed network superimposed on an existing computer network.

The macvlan driver connects Docker containers directly to the host machine's physical network. It assigns a unique MAC address to a container, rendering it a virtual physical device on the network. This driver is ideal for modernizing legacy apps requiring direct physical network connection.

Here's a simple image that provides an overview of Docker's network drivers and their primary purposes.

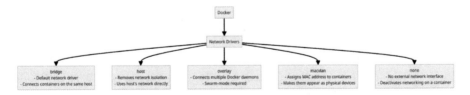

Figure 4-1. *Overview of docker network drivers*

Basic Docker Networking Commands

Docker offers various commands for managing networks. We can list, create, connect, disconnect, inspect, and remove Docker networks using these commands.

Table 4-1. *Docker networking commands*

Command	Description
docker network connect	Connects a container to a network
docker network create	Creates a new network
docker network disconnect	Disconnects a container from a network
docker network inspect	Displays detailed network information

To sum up, Docker's three primary network drivers are bridge, host, and none. The host driver leverages the host machine's networking, while the none driver cuts off containers from the external network. Then there are user-defined networks like overlay and macvlan, which support multi-host communication and are often used in environments like Docker Swarm or Kubernetes.

Docker Volumes

Docker volumes play a pivotal role in efficiently managing data within containers. First of all, let us understand what Docker volume is. A Docker volume is just a directory that lives outside of a container's file system, yet it is available to the container. It allows data to persist even when the container is halted or deleted. They enable persistent and shareable data among containers, effectively separating application data from the underlying infrastructure. Volumes provide a bridge through which data can exist and survive independently of the containers using them. This fundamental distinction offers several advantages:

- **Persistence across container restarts**: Containers are temporary, with their data typically lost upon restart. Docker Volumes address this challenge by persisting data even as containers come and go.

- **Isolation and portability**: Volumes decouple data from containers, enhancing isolation and simplifying the sharing and transporting of data between different environments.

- **Data sharing**: Containers can share data through volumes, allowing multiple containers to access the same dataset concurrently. It enables microservices architectures and other scenarios where data must be shared between containers.

Getting Started with Docker Volumes

Volumes are stored in a part of the host filesystem managed by Docker (/var/lib/docker/volumes/ on Linux by default).

Figure 4-2. *Docker volume flow*

In this diagram:

- The **Docker Engine** runs on the **Docker Host** and manages containers and volumes.

- **Containers A** and **B** represent Docker containers running on the same Docker host.

- **Docker Volume A** and **Docker Volume B** are volumes created by the Docker Engine.

- These volumes persist data on the **Host File System**, independent of the life cycle of the containers.

- The containers read from and write data to these volumes, ensuring data persistence and consistency.

Creating Docker Volumes

Creating Docker volumes is easy. Use the docker volume create command followed by your desired volume name. For example, running `docker volume create mydata` produces a volume named "mydata." Volumes may also be created at container-creation time using the -v flag.

Listing Available Volumes

Run the command `docker volume ls` to see all volumes available on our system. This will provide much-needed information about each volume including its name, unique ID, and the driver used for management.

Volume Inspection

To fully understand a Docker volume, explore its details with the `docker volume inspect` command and append the name of your volume. It shows comprehensive details about the configuration and how the volume is stored in our host system.

Mounting Data Volumes

One of the most distinguishing features of Docker volumes is their ability to be mounted in containers. This smooth interaction allows data to easily pass between containers. When starting up a container, one ensures that all the stored data in the volume is easily accessed.

```
$ docker run -d -v mydata:/app/data myapp
```

This command mounts the "mydata" volume to the "/app/data" directory within the container named "myapp."

Copy Containers Data

Docker volumes facilitate the easy transfer of files and directories between containers. Utilize the `docker cp` command to copy data from one container to another without complications. It is very useful when one wants to transfer specific data without exposing the entire volume.

Host Directories As Data Volumes

Besides creating and managing internal Docker volumes, we can also include the host directories as volumes within the containers. This way presents a convenient means to work on data that resides on the host system while capitalizing on the containerized environment.

Ownership and Permissions of Volumes

Understanding volume permissions and ownership plays a crucial role in managing the data within containers. By default, data within a container remains with the permissions it has in the volume directory. We can also include user and group IDs with this to control the owner within the container.

Deleting Docker Volumes

When volumes are no longer in use, `docker volume rm` and the name of the volume make their deletion easier. However, this also includes the deletion of the data stored in the volumes and should be exercised with care.

Bulk Volume Deletion

In cases where more than one volume needs to be removed, the command `docker volume prune` steps in. This command deletes all volumes that are unlinked from running and stopped containers.

The following diagram visually represents creating a Docker volume, mounting it within a container, and using it to store and access data. Following is the explanation in detail:

1. **Create volume:** A Docker volume is created on the host system using the `docker volume create` command or during container creation using the `-v` flag.

2. **Mount in container:** The created Docker volume is mounted within a container during its launch, ensuring data sharing.

3. **Access and store data:** The container can access and store data within the mounted Docker volume. Multiple containers can share the same volume.

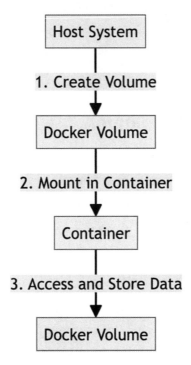

Figure 4-3. *Docker volumes in action*

In a nutshell, Docker volumes provide an effective means of managing container data. It empowers the persistence of data, facilitates sharing, and ensures effective communication between containers and the host system. Equipped with the knowledge of creating, managing, and utilizing volumes efficiently, we can amplify the versatility and efficiency of our containerized applications.

Docker Compose

Understanding Docker Compose

Docker Compose simplifies the management of multicontainer applications, making it an excellent tool for Java developers. We can seamlessly orchestrate complex setups by defining services, networks, and volumes in a single file. Whether working on a Spring Boot application or any Java project, Docker Compose enhances our development workflow. With Docker Compose, Java developers can efficiently create, configure, and manage multicontainer applications.

Docker Compose simplifies the management of multicontainer applications by defining them in a single `docker-compose.yml` file. This file can include services, networks, and volumes, making it a convenient tool for orchestrating complex setups. Like the Dockerfile, this file should also be placed at the root of our project repository.

Here's a simple diagram illustrating the basic structure of a Docker Compose file.

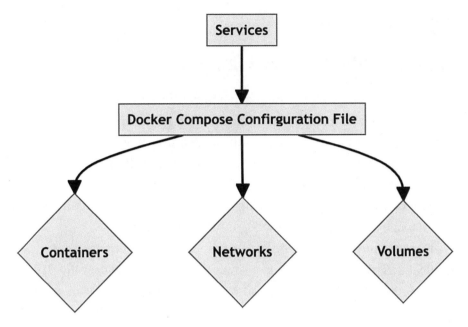

Figure 4-4. *Docker compose file components*

Docker Compose File Components

In this diagram, each component is represented separately, showing its relationship to the Docker Compose configuration:

- Services are the fundamental building blocks defining the containers, their configurations, and their interaction. A service is a definition for a containerized application or a microservice within a Docker Compose configuration.

- Docker Compose configuration file, that is, `docker-compose.yaml`, connects three different components: "Containers," "Networks," and "Volumes." It serves as a central configuration file that outlines how these components are defined and how they interact.

Setting Up Docker Compose

Obtaining Docker Compose in the most straightforward and advisable manner involves installing Docker Desktop, a complete package containing Docker Compose, Docker Engine, and Docker CLI—essential components for Compose.

Docker Desktop is available on Linux, Mac, and Windows. If Docker Desktop is already installed, finding the installed version of Compose can be found by selecting "About Docker Desktop" from the whale icon on the Docker menu.

Figure 4-5. *Verifying docker compose installation*

We can also verify the installation by running the following command.

```
$ docker-compose --version
```

Docker Compose in Action

Let's understand how docker compose works.

- **Defining services with docker compose**: Services
  in Docker Compose are equivalent to individual
  containers. Define services in the `docker-compose.yml`
  file under the `services` section. For a Java application,
  we might define a service for the application and
  another for the database.

  Example of defining a Java application service:

```
version: '3'
services:
  app:
    build: .
    ports:
      - "8080:8080"
    environment:
      SPRING_DATASOURCE_URL: jdbc:mysql://db:3306/mydb
      SPRING_DATASOURCE_USERNAME: user
      SPRING_DATASOURCE_PASSWORD: password
    depends_on:
      - db
  db:
    image: mysql:5.7
    environment:
      MYSQL_ROOT_PASSWORD: root
      MYSQL_DATABASE: mydb
      MYSQL_USER: user
      MYSQL_PASSWORD: password
```

Service for Java Application

- **Networking in docker compose**: Docker Compose
  automatically creates a network for our services,
  allowing them to communicate using service names
  as hostnames. This simplifies networking for Java
  applications that need to connect to databases or other
  services.

- **Managing dependencies and startup order**: The
  depends_on directive ensures that services start in the
  correct order, helping Java applications that rely on
  databases or other services.

- **Environment variables and secrets**: Environment
  variables can be set in the docker-compose.yml
  file or separate .env files. This is useful for passing
  configurations to Java applications without modifying
  the source code.

Here in the following code under environment tag,
we have declared env variables for the Spring Boot
application:

```
version: '3'
services:
  app:
    build: .
    ports:
      - "8080:8080"
    environment:
      SPRING_DATASOURCE_URL: jdbc:mysql://db:3306/mydb
      SPRING_DATASOURCE_USERNAME: user
      SPRING_DATASOURCE_PASSWORD: password
```

Envrionment variables

- **Scaling services**: Scaling services is very easy with Docker Compose. Define the desired scale for a service, and Docker Compose will create and manage multiple instances.

We can use the `--scale` flag to specify the number of instances you want for a service:

```
$docker-compose up --scale web=3
```

If you are using Docker Swarm, the `deploy.replicas` directive will specify the desired number of instances, or replicas, for a service.

```
version: '3'
services:
  app:
    image: openjdk:17
    # ...
    deploy:
      replicas: 3
```

Scaling Services using Docker Swarm

When using `docker stack deploy` and deploying a stack in Swarm mode, Docker will create the number of replicas of the specified service.

```
$docker stack deploy -c docker-compose.yml mystack
```

This command uses the `deploy.replicas` setting to manage the scale of the service.

Docker Compose Support in Spring Boot

Spring Boot 3.1 has introduced an exciting feature: built-in support for Docker Compose. This addition significantly simplifies the development process for Spring Boot applications that rely on Docker for environment setup. Before Spring Boot 3.1, using Docker Compose involved manually running `docker compose up` to start services, followed by `docker compose down` to stop them. This required developers to manage Docker Compose separately and ensure their Spring Boot application's configuration aligned with the dynamically assigned ports and service settings.

With Spring Boot 3.1, this process is streamlined. Spring Boot can now automatically detect a `docker-compose.yaml` file and manage the life cycle of Docker Compose services directly. This means:

- Spring Boot runs `docker compose up` automatically before connecting to services.

- If the services are already running, Spring Boot uses them as they are.

- Upon shutting down, the application `docker compose stop` is executed, preventing lingering Docker containers.

The integration builds on the `ConnectionDetails` abstraction. Spring Boot automatically detects images started by Docker Compose and creates `ConnectionDetails` beans pointing to these services. This eliminates the need for manual configuration in many cases.

Moreover, support for Docker Compose has been integrated into start.spring.io, accelerating your project setup process!

- We can create a new project with the "Docker Compose support" option.

Figure 4-6. *Add Docker Compose support dependency*

- And including dependencies like the "PostgreSQL driver," you automatically receive a well-configured `compose.yaml` file at no extra cost.

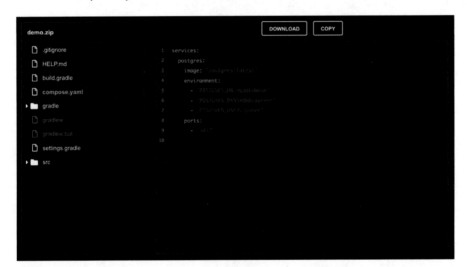

Figure 4-7. *Preconfigured compose.yaml*

How amazing is that!

Integrating Docker Compose into Spring Boot is a significant step in simplifying Spring Boot application development workflow. It allows developers to focus more on building their applications and less on configuring their development environment.

Summary

This chapter has covered advanced Docker concepts: networking, volumes, and compose. We have examined network drivers like bridge, host, none, and user-defined networks and also learned about basic networking commands.

For Docker volumes, we learned how they can be used for persistence and sharing between containers. This chapter showed how to create, list, and inspect volumes, mount them, and manage permissions and ownership; how to delete volumes was also shown.

We then covered Docker Compose, which manages multicontainer applications. We also explained the structure of docker-compose.yml files and topics such as defining services, networking, managing dependencies, and scaling. The chapter concluded by providing an overview of Docker Compose support in Spring Boot 3.1, which improves integration and development workflows. Knowing these features will help in development and deploying containerized applications.

In the next chapter, we will learn about various base images we can use for containerizing Java applications.

CHAPTER 5

Containerizing Java Applications with Dockerfile

This chapter will take a much deeper look at containerizing Java applications with Docker with a specific focus on Spring Boot. The key topics will include selection of base image for a Dockerfile and brief intro to buildpack for containerizing Spring Boot applications.

Understanding Base Images

A proper base image is crucial while working with Docker for Java applications. A base image is referred to as the foundation on which your application will be built. The base image holds the essential OS and runtime environment that your application needs to run. Therefore, the choice of a base image has a severe impact on many aspects, including size, compatibility, security, and performance.

There are several essential considerations when selecting a base image for your Java application. Let's consider those and the options you have when determining a good base image.

Figure 5-1. *Java inside a docker container*

Choosing JDK vs. JRE As the Base Image

When choosing a base image for your Java application, you can select either JDK or JRE as your base image. Let's explore the differences between the two:

Aspect	JDK Base Image	JRE Base Image
Includes	Full Java development environment, including compiler and tools required for development.	Only the runtime environment is required to execute Java applications.
Use Case	Suitable for building and compiling Java applications within the Docker image.	Suitable for deploying Java applications without development tools.
Development vs. Production	Chosen during development or when code compilation is required within the container.	Preferred for production deployments due to reduced attack surface and smaller image size.

Official OpenJDK Images

Images of official OpenJDK versions are also available from the likes of Oracle. They can be good, safe, and well-maintained choices. Different images exist in various versions and tags; you'll get to use the exact Java version and JVM implementation your application requires.

For instance, if you're developing a Java 17 application, you can use the following Dockerfile snippet: Images.

```
FROM openjdk:17-jdk
```

This line in the Dockerfile says it uses OpenJDK image as a base. OpenJDK is an open source implementation of the Java Platform.

17-jdk indicates Java version 17, which is an LTS or a Long-Term Support version for Java, and the image contains the complete Java Development Kit, ready for compiling and building Java applications.

Eclipse Temurin Images

The Eclipse Temurin project provides a range of Docker images for different Java versions and JVM implementations. These images are community-supported and can be a good choice if you need specific features or optimizations. For example, you can use AdoptOpenJDK's images with Java 17:

```
FROM eclipse-temurin:17-jdk
```

Specifies the Eclipse Temurin project image as the base. Eclipse Temurin provides high-quality, vendor-neutral builds of OpenJDK.

Alpine Linux Images

Alpine Linux is a slim distro mainly used to create small Docker images. If you use Alpine Linux as your base image, your image size will significantly reduce, making your application download and deploy much faster.

Here's an example of using Alpine Linux with OpenJDK 17:

```
FROM eclipse-temurin:17-alpine
```

Eclipse Temurin provides builds of the OpenJDK. Here Alpine refers to the Alpine Linux variant of the image. It is a lightweight distribution, making the image smaller and more secure.

Distroless Base Images

Distroless is a Google project that creates minimal base images that favors security and simplicity. The images don't include the package managers or shells that are traditionally part of a Linux distribution; therefore, they are smaller and more secure. These images reduce the attack surface for the applications. These images are even smaller than alpine linux images.

The idea here is that you keep only the stuff relevant to your applications and get rid of the bloat. Since they are small in size, it makes perfect sense to use them for cloud use cases because in the cloud you are being charged heavily for the computing resources.

Consider the following Distroless example for your Java application:

```
FROM gcr.io/distroless/java:17
```

Building Custom Base Images

Sometimes, you might need to create a custom base image tailored to your application's requirements. This can include adding specific libraries, tools, or configurations your application depends on.

Here's a simplified example of creating a custom base image with additional dependencies:

```
FROM eclipse-temurin:17-jdk AS base
# Add any common dependencies
FROM base AS build
COPY . /app
WORKDIR /app
RUN ./gradlew build
FROM base AS final
COPY --from=build /app/build/libs/my-app.jar /app.jar
CMD ["java", "-jar", "/app.jar"]
```

Multi-stage Builds for Optimization

Multi-stage builds help optimize your final image size by separating the build and runtime environments. This reduces unnecessary dependencies in the final image. Multi-stage Docker builds are ideal for creating smaller, more secure images. This approach enhances reproducibility and reduces image size.

Here, the idea is that we build application-specific artifacts in the first stage of the build and then insert them into our final runtime image.

Here's an example of a multi-stage Dockerfile for containerizing Spring Boot applications:

```
FROM maven:3.9.4-eclipse-temurin-17 AS build
COPY . /app
WORKDIR /app
RUN mvn clean package
FROM eclipse-temurin:17-jre
COPY --from=build /app/target/my-app.jar /app.jar
CMD ["java", "-jar", "/app.jar"]
```

Security Considerations

Choose a base image as close as possible to the officially maintained repositories, and keep updated as often as necessary in your CI/CD pipeline so you will receive security patches and fixes. Explore scanning your Docker images for vulnerabilities through tools like Clair or Trivy.

Clair is an open source static analysis tool for container images that can parse image contents and report vulnerabilities affecting the container images.

Trivy is another open source security scanner tool that can find vulnerabilities and misconfigurations across:

- Code repositories

- Binary artifacts

- Container images

- Kubernetes clusters

The correct choice of a base image is important while Dockerizing your Java applications. Compatibility, size of the image, and security play a key role in deciding a base image. With a clear understanding of base images and alternatives such as Distroless, developers get well prepared to build and deploy Java applications using Docker more effectively.

Containerizing and Running a Spring Boot Application

Dockerizing a Spring Boot Application

There are many advantages of running your Spring Boot application in a Docker container.

- First of all, developing in Docker is easy because it has a user-friendly CLI-based workflow that lets anyone develop, share, and run their containerized Spring applications flawlessly.

- Second, Docker streamlines installation; developers can use one package to deploy an application quickly.

- Last but not least, Docker ensures consistency between the development and production environments; developers can code and test locally.

Containerizing a Spring Boot application is straightforward. You can achieve this by placing the `.jar` or `.war` file directly into a JDK base image and then package it into a Docker image. While numerous online resources are available to guide you through this process, many crucial aspects, such as Docker image security, image size optimization, proper tagging, and efficient build performance, often go unaddressed. This lesson will address these common concerns and provide nine valuable tips for containerizing your Spring Boot application.

Building a Simple Spring Boot Application

To illustrate the importance of addressing these concerns, let's start by building a basic "Hello World" Spring Boot application. To create this application, we will begin by downloading a pre-initialized project using Spring Initializr, generating a ZIP file, and following a few simple steps to run the application.

Under the directory `src/main/java/com/helloworld/`, you can modify the `HelloWorldApplication.java` file. This file will contain the following code:

```java
package com.example.helloworld;
import org.springframework.boot.SpringApplication;
import org.springframework.boot.autoconfigure.
SpringBootApplication;
import org.springframework.web.bind.annotation.RequestMapping;
import org.springframework.web.bind.annotation.RestController;
@RestController
@SpringBootApplication
public class HelloWorldApplication {
    @RequestMapping("/")
    public String home() {
        return "Hello World!";
    }
    public static void main(String[] args) {
        SpringApplication.run(HelloWorldApplication.
        class, args);
    }
}
```

To package your compiled code into a distributable format, such as a JAR, use the following commands:

```
$ ./mvnw package
$ java -jar target/*.jar
```

You should now be able to access the "Hello World" application at http://localhost:8080 through your web browser or via curl.

```
$ curl localhost:8080
Hello World!
```

To Dockerize this application, you'll need a Dockerfile. A Dockerfile is a text document that contains instructions for assembling a Docker image. Each instruction corresponds to a layer in the Docker image. Typically, developers use the following Dockerfile template:

```
FROM eclipse-temurin:17-jdk
ARG JAR_FILE=target/*.jar
COPY ${JAR_FILE} app.jar
EXPOSE 8080
ENTRYPOINT ["java", "-jar", "/app.jar"]
```

- The first line defines the base image.

- The ARG instruction specifies variables available to the COPY instruction.

- The COPY instruction copies the JAR file from the target/ folder to the root of your Docker image.

- The EXPOSE instruction informs Docker about the container's network port.

- Finally, the ENTRYPOINT command configures the container to run as an executable, equivalent to running the java -jar target/*.jar command.

Build the Docker image using the following command:

```
$ docker build -t spring-boot-helloworld .
```

Finally, run the container with docker run command.

```
$ docker run -p 8080:8080 -t spring-boot-helloworld
```

However, a limitation of this approach is that you must create a JAR file on the host system using the ./mvnw package command, which necessitates manual Java installation, configuration of the JAVA_HOME environment variable, and Maven installation. The JDK must reside outside the Docker container, adding complexity to the build environment.

We can automate the JAR file creation during the image's build to resolve this.

```
FROM eclipse-temurin:jdk-17
WORKDIR /app
COPY .mvn/ .mvn
COPY mvnw pom.xml ./
RUN ./mvnw dependency:go-offline

COPY src ./src
CMD ["./mvnw", "spring-boot:run"]
```

Containerizing Spring Boot Application with Buildpack

Spring Boot 2.3 has come with an exciting new feature: buildpack support, where we can use an effortlessly created Docker image instead of having to craft our own Dockerfile and execute complex commands using docker build from the command line. All that will now be required is a simple command:

```
$ mvn spring-boot:build-image
```

Likewise, for Gradle enthusiasts:

```
$ ./gradlew bootBuildImage
```

It is important to note that these commands can only be executed correctly when Docker is installed and running on our system. The build-image goal greatly simplifies the process by completely automating the creation and the rapid deployment of Docker images, so developers no longer need to manually craft a Dockerfile or deal with especially complex build commands. This process abstracts away a number of the underlying complexities. It provides a cloud-like deployment experience comparable to a few platforms such as Heroku or Cloud Foundry.

This approach further revolutionizes how to construct Docker images. Rather than having to make the same change in multiple Dockerfiles across different projects, we can craft or customize the image builder of buildpacks for our use cases.

Apart from the obvious simplicity and improved developer experience, buildpacks can significantly enhance efficiency. For instance, the buildpacks approach naturally results in a layered Docker image, and it takes advantage of the exploded version of the JAR file.

Summary

This chapter focuses on containerizing Spring Boot Java applications using Docker. It starts by exploring base images, from which all Docker containers begin: options are diverse, from an official OpenJDK image down to very lightweight Alpine Linux versions.

Next, we learned about Dockerizing a simple "Hello World" Spring Boot application: steps to wrap the application in a Docker container. You also developed some understanding of advanced topics like multi-stage builds and security recommendations for your Docker images using Distroless images.

One very notable feature is buildpacks, which Spring Boot 2.3 now offers. This will allow you to use Docker images without writing a single Dockerfile: with just a simple command, you are good to go. That makes the containerization process much easier.

## CHAPTER 6

Working with Container Builder Tools for Java Applications

This chapter will take a much deeper look at four main tools: Google Jib, Fabric8 Docker Maven Plugin, Spotify's Docker-Maven-Plugin, and Cloud-Native Buildpacks. Each tool approaches Java application containerization differently, from streamlining Docker image creation to integrating seamlessly with Maven build processes.

Building Container Images with the Google Jib

Understanding Jib

Google Jib is the Java containerizer developed by Google, and it's actually tailor-made for Java developers. What distinguishes Jib from others is its simplicity. Google Jib simplifies creating a container image for Java developers: abstracting away the complexities of Docker so that developers can focus on their artifacts. Jib's intelligent layering and use of distroless images make the containerization process efficient and secure.

Following are some of the key features of Jib:

- Jib eliminates the need for developers to know about Docker installation.

- Jib operates without a daemon.

- Jib doesn't require a Dockerfile.

- Jib doesn't engage with Docker's complexities, such as the docker build, tag, and push processes.

- With Jib to containerize your Java application, a Java developer can add a Jib plugin to their chosen build tool (Maven or Gradle), and that's all that's required.

- Jib intelligently divides your application into multiple layers. When code changes occur, only the affected layers are rebuilt, significantly reducing build times.

Jib accepts your application's source code as input and generates a container image for your application as output.

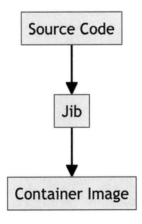

Figure 6-1. *Jib in action*

Building with Jib

A Java application image is normally represented by one layer containing the application JAR. However, Jib uses a special build approach, breaking an application into multiple layers. This kind of splitting allows for even more finely grained incremental builds. Thus, changing some code rebuilds only those parts you have changed and does not involve other parts of the application. These layers are placed, by default, over an OpenJDK base image; otherwise, you can also configure a custom base image.

In your `pom.xml`file, you can configure the Maven Jib plugin for Spring Boot projects. Below is a sample configuration:

```
<project>
  ...
  <build>
    <plugins>
      ...
      <plugin>
        <groupId>com.google.cloud.tools</groupId>
        <artifactId>jib-maven-plugin</artifactId>
        <version>3.3.2</version>
        <configuration>
          <to>
            <image>docker.io/my-docker-id/my-app</image>
          </to>
        </configuration>
      </plugin>
      ...
    </plugins>
  </build>
  ...
</project>
```

With the Maven Jib plugin configured, building the container image is as simple as running a Maven command:

```
mvn compile jib:build
```

This command compiles your project, constructs the Docker image, and pushes it to the specified container registry.

For Gradle-based projects, you include the Jib Gradle plugin in your build.gradle:

```
plugins {
  id 'com.google.cloud.tools.jib' version '2.7.1'
}
jib.to.image = 'my-docker-id/my-app'
```

Use the following command to create and push an image with Gradle.

```
./gradlew jib
```

Understanding Jib Image Layering

Jib's image layering strategy allows for fine-grained control over the container image's composition, promoting incremental builds and efficient resource utilization during containerization.

Here's a breakdown of the layers created by Jib:

1. **Dependencies layer**: This layer includes the external modules and libraries used by the application. This ensures that dependencies are independent and cacheable separately and that reusability in builds is enhanced.

2. **Resources layer**: In the resources layer, Jib includes
    application resources like configuration files,
    templates, and static assets. These resources can be
    cached separately at the same time, thus reducing
    redundancy while building.

3. **Classes layer**: This class layer has the actual
    compiled classes of the application in Java. With
    each change in the code, only this layer needs to be
    rebuilt, which makes building a lot faster.

4. **Snapshot dependencies layer**: Jib dedicates an
    exact layer for all those dependencies that are
    occasionally changing or are the snapshots.

5. **Custom layers**: Additional directories, if any that are
    provided by the developer, usually through config
    may be turned into their layers.

This distinct layer separation helps Jib to optimize the build process by breaking down the application into these distinct layers. With changes, only the layers affected need to be rebuilt and pushed to the registry; other layers are not affected, making quicker and more efficient container image updates.

That helps to speed up the builds as well as how the resources get used. It just makes sure that only the necessary parts are rebuilt and pushed, which then keeps the size of container images themselves minimal.

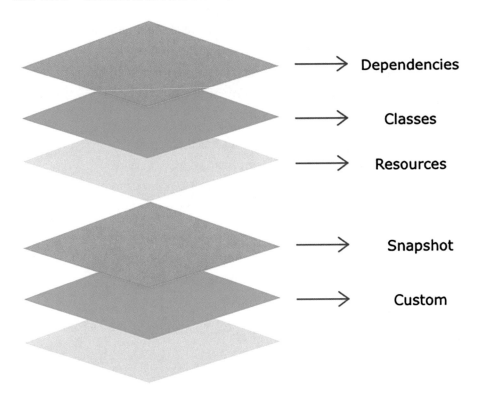

Figure 6-2. *Jib image layers*

Building Container Images with Fabric8 Docker Maven Plugin

Containers have now become the critical technology in modern software development and deployment; they ensure consistency, portability, and scalability for different applications across different environments. Again as we know Docker is the de facto standard in containerization and together with Maven provides a very smooth development workflow. This section will explore how to work with the Fabric8 Docker Maven Plugin; a solid tool invented for easy building and management of Docker images with our Maven projects.

The Fabric8 Docker Maven plugin is an open source Maven plugin to tightly integrate Docker image creation within our own Maven build process. It falls under a variety of tools by Fabric8, aimed at making Kubernetes and OpenShift easy to use by developers.

Understanding Fabric8 Docker Maven Plugin

This plugin enables developers to specify Docker image configurations directly within the Maven POM, or Project Object Model file for their project, and further build the Docker image easily.

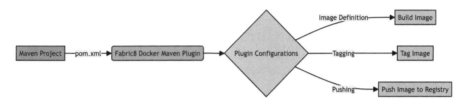

Figure 6-3. *Image build process with fabric8 docker maven plugin*

Benefits of Fabric8 Docker Maven Plugin

- **Easy setup**: The plugin allows us to maintain the Docker image configurations within our pom.xml rather than maintaining it separately in a Docker file.

- **Seamless integration**: It integrates Docker image creation into the Maven build process and so containerization becomes a smooth part of our development workflow.

- **Consistent builds**: With Maven, we ensure that the Docker images are created and versioned consistently with the Java applications.

- **Efficient development**: The plugin efficiently streamlines building and managing Docker images with huge savings of time and development efforts.

- **Docker registry support**: We can easily push our images to Docker registries for distribution and deployment.

- **Community support**: Being part of the Fabric8 ecosystem, we can get active community support in the form of continuous updates and support.

Setting Up Fabric8 Docker Maven Plugin

To get started with the Fabric8 Docker Maven Plugin, we need to include it in our project's pom.xml file. Here's how we can do it:

```
<plugin>
    <groupId>io.fabric8</groupId>
    <artifactId>docker-maven-plugin</artifactId>
    <version>[LATEST_VERSION]</version>
    <configuration>
        <!-- Plugin configuration goes here -->
    </configuration>
</plugin>
```

In this example, we've added the Fabric8 Docker Maven Plugin to the build section of the pom.xml file. It specifies the plugin's group ID, artifact ID, and version, which should match the latest version available during our project setup.

Defining Docker image configuration: The Fabric8 Docker Maven Plugin allows us to define Docker image configurations directly in our pom. xml. We can specify the base image, exposed ports, environment variables, etc. Below is a simplified example:

```xml
<configuration>
    <images>
        <image>
            <alias>my-app-image</alias>
            <name>username/my-app</name>
            <build>
                <from>openjdk:11-jre-slim</from>
                <assembly>
                    <descriptorRef>artifact</descriptorRef>
                </assembly>
            </build>
            <run>
                <ports>
                    <port>tomcat.port:8080</port>
                </ports>
                <env>
                    <SPRING_PROFILES_ACTIVE>production</SPRING_
                    PROFILES_ACTIVE>
                </env>
            </run>
        </image>
    </images>
</configuration>
```

In this configuration, we define an image with the alias my-app-image and the name my-app. The base image is set to openjdk:11-jre-slim, representing a minimalistic Java 11 runtime environment. We expose port 8080 to allow incoming connections. An environment variable SPRING_ PROFILES_ACTIVE is set to production.

Building docker image: With the Fabric8 Docker Maven Plugin configured, we can now build Docker images as part of our Maven build process. Run the following command:

```
mvn package docker:build
```

This command triggers the `docker-maven-plugin` during the `install` phase of our project's build life cycle. The plugin reads our defined configuration `pom.xml` and builds the specified Docker image accordingly.

Pushing docker image: The Fabric8 Docker Maven Plugin offers advanced features like tagging and pushing images to a registry, among others.

- To push the image to a Docker registry, specify the registry details. The registry element can be omitted if you're pushing to Docker Hub. For a custom registry, define its URL. It's recommended to define your registry credentials in the Maven `settings.xml` file rather than in `pom.xml` for security reasons.

  For example, `pom.xml` is typically part of the source code, and there is a risk of committing it to the version control system, making it difficult to remove from the commit history. This is a classic case of credential leakage.

  In your `settings.xml`:

```
<servers>
    <server>
        <id>your.registry.com</id> <!-- Use Docker Hub
        ID or your custom registry's ID -->
        <username>yourusername</username>
        <password>yourpassword</password>
    </server>
</servers>
```

- Then, in your `pom.xml` Reference the server ID:

```
<push>
    <registry>your.registry.com</registry>
    <serverId>your.registry.com</serverId>
    <!-- Matches the ID in settings.xml -->
</push>
```

- Here's an example of how to tag and push an image:

```
<configuration>
    <images>
        <image>
            <!-- Image configuration -->
            <name>username/my-app:${project.
            version}</name>
            <build>
                <!-- Build configuration -->
            </build>
            <push>
                <registry>your.registry.com</registry>
                <!-- Optional for Docker Hub -->
            </push>
        </image>
    </images>
</configuration>
```

- To define our image with the desired tag, we can use Maven properties like `${project.version}` for dynamic tagging based on our project's version. This allows us to tag our image with a particular version or label and push it to a Docker registry for distribution.

- To push the image, we can use `mvn docker:push` maven command.

The Fabric8 Docker Maven Plugin simplifies Docker image creation and management in Maven projects. With this integration and easy-to-configure options, it empowers developers to adopt containerization without all the complexity involved with Dockerfiles. So this plugin gets incorporated into our process to make efficient building and management of Docker images possible, and our applications would always be consistent and portable on containerized environments.

Building Container Images with Spotify's Docker-Maven-Plugin

While Docker provides a powerful set of commands and features for creating and managing containers, it can be challenging to integrate these tasks seamlessly into the software development process. This is where tools like Spotify's Docker-Maven-Plugin come into play, as it simplifies the build process of Java applications. This plugin seamlessly integrates Docker into your Maven build process, making it easier than ever to package your Java applications into Docker containers.

This lesson will explore the Dockerfile-Maven plugin and demonstrate how it can streamline your Java application builds.

Understanding Spotify's Docker-Maven-Plugin

The Docker-Maven-Plugin for Spotify is an open source tool aimed to simplify the process of containerizing the Java application for you, particularly when you have the build automation tool Apache Maven. The Dockerfile-Maven plugin packs the Java application into the container easily and simply by integrating Docker directly into the Maven build process so that building and maintaining containers becomes easier, particularly based on a manually created Dockerfile.

Key advantages of the Dockerfile-Maven plugin:

- **Streamlined containerization**: The Dockerfile-Maven plugin seamlessly integrates Docker into the Maven build process, simplifying the process of creating Docker containers for your Java applications.

- **Manual Dockerfile utilization**: While it doesn't generate Dockerfiles, the plugin allows you to use your manually created Dockerfile, giving you full control over container configuration and dependencies.

- **Efficient Docker image builds**: With a simple Maven command, you can efficiently build Docker images, ensuring consistency and reliability in your containerization process.

- **Saves development time**: By automating Docker image creation within your build process, the plugin reduces the need for manual intervention, saving development time and effort.

- **Integration with Maven ecosystem**: Dockerfile-Maven seamlessly integrates with the Maven ecosystem, making it a natural choice for Java developers already using Maven for their projects.

```
mvn package  # Builds Docker image
mvn deploy   # Pushes the Docker image
```

- **Customizable configuration**: You have the flexibility to customize the Docker image configuration within your project's pom.xml to match your specific application requirements.

Getting Started

Using Spotify's Docker-Maven-Plugin is straightforward:

1. **Add the plugin**: In your project's pom.xml, add the Docker-Maven-Plugin as a build plugin. Specify the image name and any other necessary configurations.

```
<plugin>
  <groupId>com.spotify</groupId>
  <artifactId>dockerfile-maven-plugin</artifactId>
  <version>${dockerfile-maven-version}</version>
  <executions>
    <execution>
      <id>default</id>
      <goals>
        <goal>build</goal>
        <goal>push</goal>
      </goals>
    </execution>
  </executions>
  <configuration>
    <repository>spotify/foobar</repository>
    <tag>${project.version}</tag>
    <buildArgs>
      <JAR_FILE>${project.build.finalName}.jar
      </JAR_FILE>
    </buildArgs>
  </configuration>
</plugin>
```

Let's break down the important part of this code snippet:

- `<executions>`: This block defines a list of executions for the plugin. In this case, there is one execution defined.

- `<execution>`: Specifies an execution within the plugin. It can have an `<id>` and a list of `<goals>`.

- `<id>`: An optional identifier for the execution. In this case, it's named `default`.

- `<goals>`: Lists the goals that will be executed within this execution. Here, two goals `build` and `push` are specified.

- `<configuration>`: This block contains configuration settings specific to the `dockerfile-maven-plugin`.`<repository>`: Specifies the name of the Docker image repository. In this example, it's set to `spotify/foobar`the repository's name where the Docker image will be stored.

- `<tag>`: Sets the tag for the Docker image. It uses the Maven variable `${project.version}` to set the tag to the project's version dynamically.

- `<buildArgs>`: Allows you to specify build arguments for the Docker image. In this case, it sets the `JAR_FILE` build argument to `${project.build.finalName}.jar`, which likely represents the name of the JAR file to include in the image.

Overall, this configuration instructs the dockerfile-maven-plugin to build a Docker image using the specified Dockerfile, tag it with the project's version, and push it to the spotify/foobar Docker image repository.

2. **Build the image**: Run a Maven build command, such as mvn package. The plugin will automatically create a Docker image of your application during the build process.

3. **Push to registry**: Using the mvn deploy command, you can push the generated Docker image to a container registry like Docker Hub or Google Container Registry. This is typically done as part of a CI/CD pipeline for production deployment.

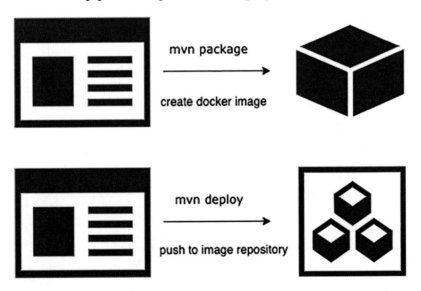

Figure 6-4. *Image build process with Spotify docker maven plugin*

Building Container Images with Cloud-Native Buildpacks

Understanding Buildpacks

Autoconfiguration revolutionized Spring. We've relied on Spring Boot's defaults to simplify configuration and boost productivity. Spring Boot autoconfiguration is a feature that facilitates the configuration of Spring applications. It's designed to minimize the manual configuration required by automatically configuring beans, settings, and components based on the dependencies in our project.

Figure 6-5. *Spring Boot autoconfiguration*

For example, when you add a dependency such as spring-boot-starter-data-jpa to your Spring Boot project, the framework recognizes the existence of classes related to JPA in the classpath and enables the relevant autoconfiguration classes like JpaRepositoriesAutoConfiguration and DataSourceAutoConfiguration. These classes automatically configure some beans like DataSource, EntityManagerFactory, and TransactionManager if they are not defined elsewhere. This process is controlled by external configuration properties, for example, spring. datasource.url, which developers can use to customize the setup. This flow streamlines the setup of complex components by applying sensible defaults but leaving room for customization.

Although these defaults usually function effectively, many view them as magical. Once we've developed our application, what about containerization? Crafting a Dockerfile that adheres to best practices for optimal containers (minimizing layers, leveraging build caches) can consume significant time, which may not be ideal for developers. Enter Cloud-Native Buildpack. CNB, like Spring's autoconfiguration, simplifies container management to mirror the simplicity Spring Boot brings to our application.

Figure 6-6. *Spring Boot buildpack*

The primary role of a buildpack is to collect all the essential components required for building and running our application. They usually operate in the background and convert our source code into a runnable application image without using Dockerfile.

Starting with Spring Boot 2.3, it uses buildpacks to generate top-tier OCI containers with effortless configuration hassle. There is no need to fret about layers, security, JVM memory calculations, or more. Create our containerized application with a single command.

Cloud-Native Buildpacks Features

Cloud-Native Buildpacks (CNBs) offer several features and capabilities for building and packaging containerized applications. Here are some of the key features supported by Cloud Native Buildpacks:

> **Dependency management**: CNBs can automatically detect and manage application dependencies, such as language runtimes, libraries, and packages. They ensure that the required dependencies are included in the application container.

Layered build: CNBs follow a layered approach to build containers. This means they create separate layers for different application parts, allowing for efficient caching and reusability during the build process.

Reproducible builds: CNBs focus on hermetic reproducible builds. This ensures that the same source code and same dependencies lead to identical container images, which is highly critical in reliability and security purposes.

Build cache: CNBs utilize a build cache in which layers that are built can be cached. This allows a cached layer to be reused as much as possible so that the build is not rebuilding everything.

Customizable builders: CNBs provide the flexibility to create custom builders tailored to specific application types or organization requirements. Custom builders can include additional buildpacks and configurations.

Life Cycle phases: The CNB build process consists of different life cycle phases, which include detection, analysis, build, and export. All these life cycle phases can be extended or customized depending on the use case.

Security scanning: CNBs often integrate with security scanning tools to identify and address vulnerabilities in application dependencies, enhancing the security of the resulting container images.

Environment variable injection: CNBs can inject environment variables into the application container, making it easy to configure runtime settings or connect to external services.

Multi-platform support: CNBs support building container images for multiple platforms and architectures, making it easier to create images that can run on different cloud providers and device types.

Compatibility: CNBs are compatible with various container runtimes and orchestrators, such as Docker, Kubernetes, and Cloud Foundry, making them versatile for different deployment scenarios.

Continuous integration (CI): CNBs can be integrated into CI/CD pipelines to automate containerization, ensuring that applications are consistently built and packaged. For example, buildpacks project offers a collection of GitHub actions for different buildpack-related activities. One of these actions allows us to configure a job prepared with the pack CLI. It's a straightforward process, and we can use this action with ease:

```
uses: buildpacks/github-actions/setup-pack@v4.1.0
```

Configuring Buildpack

Spring Boot 2.3.0.M1 introduces native buildpack support for both Maven and Gradle. This simplifies the process of generating a Docker image for our application.

- First, ensure we have a local Docker installed and running. Spring Boot buildpack integration needs a running Docker daemon. Otherwise, we get an error:

```
Failed to execute goal org.springframework.boot:
spring-boot-maven-plugin:2.4.2:build-image (default-
cli) on project imagebuilder: Execution default-
cli of goal org.springframework.boot:spring-boot-
maven-plugin:2.4.2:build-image failed: Connection to
the Docker daemon at 'localhost' failed with error
"[61] Connection refused"; ensure the Docker daemon is
running and accessible
```

  It differs from Jib in this aspect, where we don't need a docker daemon for building container images.

- Next, create a new Spring Boot project using start. spring.io.

- For Maven, we can use the command, and for Gradle, it's gradle bootBuildImage. We can swiftly create a well-configured image and store it in our local Docker daemon with a single command. It will take a little time to run the first time around, but subsequent calls will be quicker. We should see something like this in the build log:

```
[INFO] Successfully built image 'docker.io/library/
buildpack:0.0.1-SNAPSHOT'
[INFO]
[INFO] ------------------------------------------------
[INFO] BUILD SUCCESS
[INFO] ------------------------------------------------
[INFO] Total time:  01:49 min
[INFO] Finished at: 2021-02-20T01:07:08+05:30
```

- We now have an OCI-compliant container image of our
  application that:

  1. Includes necessary middleware like the JRE.

  2. Has specific customizations based on our
     application framework (Spring Boot).

  3. It was created in a disposable build container,
     provided only with the application source code.

  4. It is secure by default, running as a non-root
     user with minimal packages installed.

  5. It will be named after our application and tagged
     with its version.

- Finally, run:

  ```
  docker run --rm -p 8080:8080 imageName
  ```

  And check the output using http://localhost:8080/.

- By default, Buildpacks store the image on the local
  Docker daemon when used with Spring Boot.
  Nevertheless, we can also push our images to a
  remote container registry. We will need to make
  specific adjustments in our Maven file to enable this
  functionality.

  ```
  <project>
    <build>
      <plugins>
        <plugin>
          <groupId>org.springframework.boot
          </groupId>
          <artifactId>spring-boot-maven-plugin
          </artifactId>
  ```

```xml
                    <configuration>
                        <image>
                            <name>docker.example.com/
                            library/${project.artifactId}
                            </name>
                            <publish>true</publish>
                        </image>
                        <docker>
                            <publishRegistry>
                                <username>user</username>
                                <password>secret</password>
                                <url>https://docker.example.
                                com/v1/</url>
                                <email>user@example.
                                com</email>
                            </publishRegistry>
                        </docker>
                    </configuration>
                </plugin>
            </plugins>
        </build>
    </project>
```

Summary

This chapter explores container builder tools for Java applications, focusing on Spring Boot. It covers Google Jib, Fabric8 Docker Maven Plugin, Spotify's Docker-Maven-Plugin, and Cloud-Native Buildpacks. All of these tools provide different means through which Java applications are containerized, ranging from creating a Docker image without

Dockerfile using Jib and buildpack and integrating Docker image build into the Maven build process. The chapter provides practical examples, configuration details, and insights into the benefits of each tool. It aims to help developers choose the right containerization method for their Java projects.

## CHAPTER 7

Deploying Docker Containers Using GitHub Actions

Containerization is now a cornerstone in application deployment strategies to run the software in light, consistent, and scalable ways. Docker for Java applications makes it possible for them to run anywhere, irrespective of differences between the underlying systems. With GitHub Actions, developers can automate the building, testing, and deployment of containers.

Understanding Github Actions

GitHub Actions is an automation tool that allows us to run workflows based on events such as a push to a repository. GitHub Actions changed the face of CI/CD. It makes CI/CD easier for a Java developer by allowing automation right from their GitHub repositories: it builds, tests, and deploys automatically without human intervention. GitHub Actions can automate any type of software workflow. This simply runs a sequence of commands following particular events on a GitHub repository: push, creating a pull request, or similar actions.

© Ashish Choudhary 2025
A. Choudhary, *When Docker Meets Java*, https://doi.org/10.1007/979-8-8688-1300-9_7

Here are some key features of GitHub Actions:

- **Workflow automation**: We can automate our build, test, and deploy workflows using actions defined in YAML files within our repository.

- **Events trigger**: Workflows can be triggered by GitHub events such as push and pull requests, issues created, releases, or any other event in the GitHub webhooks payload.

- **Reusable components**: Actions can be created and shared as individual tasks, which others can use in their workflows.

- **Marketplace**: GitHub Marketplace provides a community of shared actions that can be used to automate all sorts of processes.

- **Language and platform support**: Actions support various programming languages and platforms, making them versatile for different projects.

- **Hosted runners**: GitHub provides hosted runners for Linux, Windows, and macOS, allowing you to run workflows on fresh virtual machines.

- **Self-hosted runners**: For custom environments or specific hardware requirements, we can also host our runners.

- **Matrix builds**: We can test across multiple operating systems, versions, or environments by defining a matrix of different configurations.

- **Secrets management**: We can store and use secrets, like API keys or credentials, securely in our workflows.

- **Artifacts and raches**: We can upload artifacts from our workflows or cache dependencies to speed up the build process.

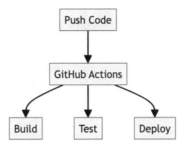

Figure 7-1. *GitHub Actions*

GitHub Action Components

Let's break down the critical elements of GitHub Actions:

- **Workflow**: It's a set of instructions to compile, test, package, or deploy code on GitHub. Defined in a YAML file within the `.github/workflows` folder of our repository, a workflow activates through specific events and comprises jobs.

- **Events**: These are the triggers for workflows. Any activity, like a push to a branch or a new pull request, can initiate the workflow.

- **Jobs**: A job is a sequence of steps that run in a virtual environment called a runner. Jobs organize the sequence of actions and can operate simultaneously or one after the other.

- **Steps**: Each step in a job corresponds to a single action, such as retrieving the code or executing a shell command.

125

- **Actions**: Actions are predefined commands you can run during steps, like pulling your code repository or setting up a Java Development Kit.

- **Runners**: These are servers where we run workflows. GitHub provides these runners, or we can set up our own. They carry out the jobs and report the outcomes to your GitHub repository. GitHub's runners are compatible with Ubuntu Linux, Windows, and macOS.

Understanding Workflow Yaml File

The diagram below outlines the relationship between a GitHub repository, workflows, and GitHub Actions.

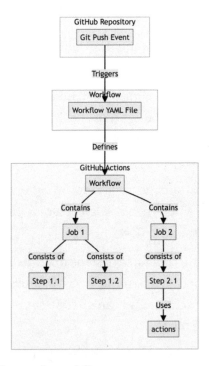

Figure 7-2. *GitHub yaml workflow*

Here's a step-by-step explanation:

GitHub repository:[Git Push Event]: This is the starting point of the workflow. A Git push event occurs when someone pushes commits to a repository on GitHub. This event can trigger a workflow.

Workflow:[Workflow YAML File]: This file, typically named main.yml or ci.yml, is located in the .github/workflows directory of your repository. It defines the workflow to be executed when the Git push event occurs.

GitHub actions:[Workflow]: This is the overall automated process defined by the workflow YAML file. It contains one or more jobs.

[Job 1] and [Job 2]: These are individual jobs within the workflow. Jobs are steps that execute on the same runner, which can run in parallel or sequentially as defined by the workflow.

[Step 1.1] and [Step 1.2]: These are steps within Job 1. Steps are individual tasks that can run commands or actions.

[Step 2.1]: This is a step within Job 2. Like the steps in Job 1, it can run commands or actions.

[actions]: This represents actions used in steps. GitHub Actions can use pre-built actions created by the community or custom ones defined in your repository.

The diagram's arrows show the direction of the workflow:

|Triggers|: The Git push event triggers the workflow defined in the workflow YAML file.

|Defines|: The workflow YAML file represents the actual workflow process.

|Contains|: The workflow contains Job 1 and Job 2.

|Consists of|: Job 1 consists of Step 1.1 and Step 1.2.

|Uses |: Step 2.1 It uses one or more actions to perform its tasks.

The above diagram shows how a Git push event triggers a defined workflow in the repository, which then controls the execution of jobs and steps through actions within the GitHub Actions environment.

Building Java Application Using Github Actions

Setting Up a Java Project

Let's discuss how to create a Java application build pipeline using GitHub Actions. Before we begin with GitHub Actions, make sure you have a Java project on GitHub. For this example, we will use a simple Java application built with Maven.

First, you need to define the workflow. Workflows are custom automated processes we set up in your repository to build, test, package, or deploy any code project on GitHub.

1. In our GitHub repository, navigate to the Actions tab. Click Java with Maven template or set up a workflow yourself.

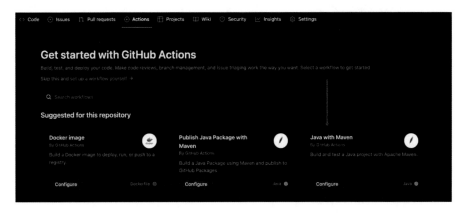

Figure 7-3. *Setting up actions*

2. This opens the workflow editor. Here, we write our
    build steps.

```
# This workflow will build a Java project with Maven,
and cache/restore any dependencies to improve the
workflow execution time
name: Java CI with Maven
on:
  push:
    branches: [ "main" ]
  pull_request:
    branches: [ "main" ]
jobs:
  build:
    runs-on: ubuntu-latest
    steps:
    - uses: actions/checkout@v3
    - name: Set up JDK 17
      uses: actions/setup-java@v3
```

```
   with:
     java-version: '17'
     distribution: 'temurin'
     cache: maven
 - name: Build with Maven
   run: mvn -B package --file pom.xml
```

Workflow file

3. Testing is a crucial aspect of the CI process. We
   should incorporate tests in our workflow to ensure
   code quality:

```
 - name: Test with Maven
   run: mvn test
```

This step runs after the build and executes all unit
tests in the project.

4. Building and testing can be time-consuming,
   primarily due to dependencies. To speed up the
   process, cache the dependencies:

```
 - name: Cache Maven packages
   uses: actions/cache@v2
   with:
     path: ~/.m2
     key: ${{ runner.os }}-m2-${{ hashFiles
     ('**/pom.xml') }}
     restore-keys: ${{ runner.os }}-m2
```

This caches the Maven packages, reducing the need
to fetch them for every build.

5.   Commit changes. This will trigger the workflow.

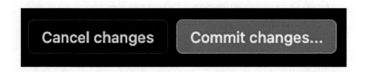

Figure 7-4. *Committing changes*

6.   Workflow completed.

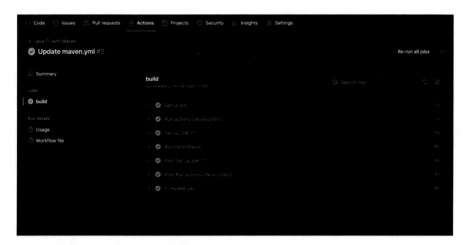

Figure 7-5. *Workflow completion*

Remember, although the guide describes a minimal Java application with Maven, there is still a lot of flexibility within GitHub Actions. Tailor the instructions to the requirements of different build tools or deployment targets. Then take full advantage of the power of automation for your Java projects.

Containerizing Java Application Using Docker GitHub Action

Let us go through the steps to containerize a Java application using GitHub Actions and Docker.

Understanding the Process

This process starts with a Dockerfile for the Java application, defining the environment and instructions to build a container image. Lastly, GitHub Actions workflows are defined to automate the execution of this process every time any change is pushed to the repository.

Figure 7-6. *GitHub Action docker flow*

Writing a Dockerfile

A Dockerfile is a script with various commands to create a Docker image. For a Java application, a typical Dockerfile might look something like this:

```
# Use a base JDK image from Docker Hub
FROM openjdk:17-jdk
# Set the working directory inside the container
WORKDIR /app
# Copy the Maven build file and source code
COPY pom.xml .
COPY src /app/src
# Build the application
RUN mvn clean package
# Expose the port the application runs on
```

```
EXPOSE 8080
# Run the jar file
CMD ["java", "-jar", "target/myapp-1.0-SNAPSHOT.jar"]
```

Setting Up Github Actions

GitHub Actions is an automation tool that allows us to run workflows based on events such as a push to a repository. Adding GitHub Actions to our Java application requires creating the directory `.github/workflows` in our repository and placing within it a YAML file describing our workflow:

```
name: Java CI with Docker
on:
  push:
    branches: [ main ]
jobs:
  build:
    runs-on: ubuntu-latest
    steps:
    - uses: actions/checkout@v2
    - name: Set up JDK 17
      uses: actions/setup-java@v2
      with:
        java-version: '17'
        distribution: 'adopt'

    - name: Build with Maven
      run: mvn clean install

    - name: Build Docker Image
      run: docker build -t my-java-app .
```

```
- name: Push Docker Image to Registry
  run: |
    echo ${{ secrets.DOCKER_HUB_PASSWORD }} | docker login
    -u ${{ secrets.DOCKER_HUB_USERNAME }} --password-stdin
    docker tag my-java-app ${{ secrets.DOCKER_HUB_USERNAME
    }}/my-java-app:latest
```

GitHub action docker workflow yaml file

This workflow does the following:

Checkout code: Grabs the latest code from the main branch.

```
- uses: actions/checkout@v2
```

Set up jdk: Configures the JDK for the runner environment.

```
- name: Set up JDK 17
  uses: actions/setup-java@v2
  with:
    java-version: '17'
    distribution: 'adopt'
```

Build with maven: Compiles the Java application and runs any tests.

```
- name: Build with Maven
  run: mvn clean install
```

Build docker image: Constructs the Docker image using the Dockerfile.

```
- name: Build Docker Image
  run: docker build -t my-java-app .
```

Push to docker registry: After the image is successfully created, it's tagged and then pushed to Docker Hub.

```
- name: Push Docker Image to Registry
  run: |
    echo ${{ secrets.DOCKER_HUB_PASSWORD }} | docker login
    -u ${{ secrets.DOCKER_HUB_USERNAME }} --password-stdin
    docker tag my-java-app ${{ secrets.DOCKER_HUB_USERNAME
    }}/my-java-app:latest
    docker push ${{ secrets.DOCKER_HUB_USERNAME }}/my-java-
    app:latest
```

The `${{ secrets.DOCKER_HUB_USERNAME }}` and `${{ secrets.DOCKER_HUB_PASSWORD }}` are GitHub secrets that you set in your repository settings for secure authentication to the Docker registry.

By containerizing your Java application using GitHub Actions and Docker, you automate your build and deployment process, which enhances productivity and reduces the chance of human error. This CI/CD approach ensures our development team can focus on what they do best—writing code not worrying about deployment intricacies. Moreover, the portability of Docker ensures that the Java application can be run on any machine without the "it works on my machine" syndrome.

Deploying Java Application to GCP Using GitHub Action

In simple terms, CI/CD automation essentially bridges your code repository to a live production environment. For Java developers, application deployment to Google Cloud Platform (GCP) just got easier using GitHub Actions and Docker. Prior knowledge of GCP is required to proceed further.

Understanding the Workflow

Before we dive into the deployment process, let's understand the workflow:

- **Code commit**: Developers push code to a GitHub repository.

- **GitHub Actions trigger**: A push event triggers the GitHub Actions workflow.

- **Build**: GitHub Actions executes a workflow that builds a Docker image.

- **Push to container registry**: The Docker image is pushed to the Google Container Registry (GCR).

- **Deploy to GCP**: The image in GCR is then deployed to a GCP service like Google Kubernetes Engine (GKE) or Google Cloud run.

Here is a diagram representing CI/CD flow with Docker, GitHub Actions, and GCP.

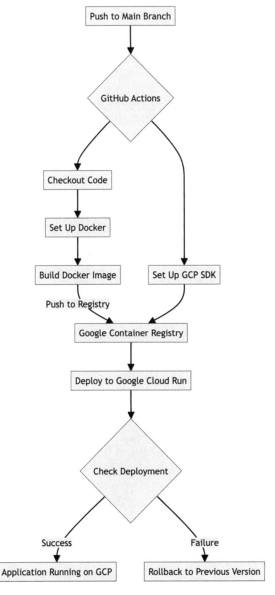

Figure 7-7. *GitHub Actions with GCP*

Setting Up the Workflow

To configure this workflow:

1. To deploy a Docker image to Google Cloud Platform (GCP) using GitHub Actions, you'll need to enable specific GCP APIs to facilitate the integration. Navigate to GCP Console and ensure that the following required Google Cloud APIs are enabled:

   - Cloud Run run.googleapis.com

   - Artifact Registry artifactregistry.googleapis.com

2. Create and configure Workload Identity Federation for GitHub (`https://github.com/google-github-actions/auth#setting-up-workload-identity-federation`).

3. Ensure the required IAM permissions are granted: Cloud Run

   - roles/run.admin

   - roles/iam.serviceAccountUser (to act as the Cloud Run runtime service account)

   Artifact Registry

   - roles/artifactregistry.admin (project or repository level)

Note   You should always follow the principle of least privilege when assigning IAM roles.

---

4. Create GitHub secrets for `WIF_PROVIDER` and `WIF_SERVICE_ACCOUNT`.

5. Change the values for the `GAR_LOCATION`, `SERVICE`, and `REGION` environment variables.

Let's begin.

Step 1: Firstly, our Java application needs to be ready for deployment. This typically involves:

- Ensuring your application is thoroughly tested and stable

- Configuring your `pom.xml` or `build.gradle` file for a successful build

Step 2: For deploying a Java application, you may need to set up various GCP resources such as a Compute Engine instance, App Engine, or Kubernetes Engine. The choice depends on your application's requirements.

- **Compute engine**: Ideal for applications requiring custom virtual machines.

- **App engine**: Suitable for applications that scale automatically.

- **Kubernetes engine**: Best for containerized applications.

- **Cloud run**: It is a managed platform that enables you to run stateless containers that are invocable via web requests or Pub/Sub events.

Step 3: Finally, we need to set up GitHub Actions so that we automate our deployment workflow. Here's how we can set it up:

- In your GitHub repository, create a `.github/workflows` directory.

- Add a workflow file (e.g., `deploy.yml`) in this directory.

```
    - name: Google Auth
jobs:
  deploy:
    # Add 'id-token' with the intended permissions for
    workload identity federation
    permissions:
      contents: 'read'
      id-token: 'write'
    runs-on: ubuntu-latest
    steps:
      - name: Checkout
        uses: actions/checkout@v2
      - name: Set up JDK
        uses: actions/setup-java@v2
        with:
          java-version: '17'
env:
  PROJECT_ID: YOUR_PROJECT_ID # TODO: update Google
  Cloud project id
  GAR_LOCATION: YOUR_GAR_LOCATION # TODO: update
  Artifact Registry location
  SERVICE: YOUR_SERVICE_NAME # TODO: update Cloud Run
  service name
  REGION: YOUR_SERVICE_REGION # TODO: update Cloud Run
  service region
on:
  push:
    branches: [ "main" ]
name: Build and Deploy to GCP Cloud Run
```

This workflow does the following:

- Triggers on a push to the main branch.

- Sets up Java environment.

- Authenticates with GCP using secrets.

- Builds a Docker image and pushes it to the Google artifact repository.

- Deploys the image to Cloud Run using a GitHub Action specifically for Cloud Run deployment.

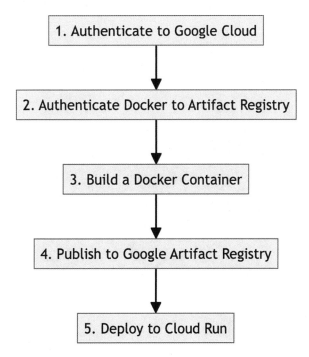

Figure 7-8. *GCP workflow*

Step 4: For security, store sensitive information like GCP credentials as encrypted secrets in your GitHub repository:

- Go to your repository's settings.

- Click on "Secrets".

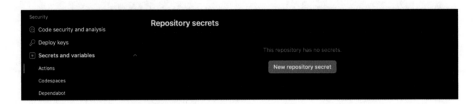

Figure 7-9. *Setting up secret*

- Add your GCP service account key and project ID as secrets.

Figure 7-10. *Creating a secret*

142

Step 5: Once the workflow is configured, any push to the main branch will trigger the deployment process. You can monitor the progress and check logs in the "Actions" tab of your repository. Remember to regularly update your workflow configurations to align with the evolving needs of your application and team.

GitHub Actions Best Practices for CI/CD with Docker

Keep Workflows DRY (Don't Repeat Yourself)

Avoid duplicated code in your GitHub Actions workflows. Reuse actions and shared logic by breaking your workflow into modular pieces. You can have reusable workflows referenced by several projects, thus reducing maintenance overhead and uniformly aligning CI/CD pipelines across the board.

Suppose you have a Java project and always run the following steps to set up a Java, build with maven, and run across different workflows. You should instead create a composite action so that you don't have to repeat these several times again for each one of your workflows.

Step 1: Create the composite action.

In your repository, create a folder structure for the composite action, like this:

```
.github/actions/java-maven-build
   ├── action.yml
```

Inside `action.yml`, define the steps you want to reuse:

```
# .github/actions/java-maven-build/action.yml
name: 'Java Maven Build'
```

```
description: 'Set up Java, build with Maven, and run tests'
runs:
  using: 'composite'
  steps:
    - name: Set up JDK 17
      uses: actions/setup-java@v3
      with:
        java-version: '17'
        distribution: 'temurin'
        cache: maven

    - name: Build with Maven
      run: mvn clean package --file pom.xml

    - name: Run Tests with Maven
      run: mvn test
```

Step 2: Reuse the composite action in your workflows.

Now that the composite action is defined, you can reuse it in multiple workflows. For instance, in your .github/workflows/main.yml:

```
name: Java CI

on:
  push:
    branches: [ main ]
  pull_request:
    branches: [ main ]

jobs:
  build:
    runs-on: ubuntu-latest
    steps:
      - uses: actions/checkout@v3
```

```
# Use the composite action
- uses: ./.github/actions/java-maven-build
```

This approach keeps your workflows DRY by consolidating repeated steps into a single composite action, making it easier to manage and update across multiple pipelines.

Use Secrets for Sensitive Information

Store sensitive data like API keys, credentials, and tokens securely in GitHub's Secrets management system. This keeps sensitive information out of your codebase and workflow files. Refer to these secrets in the workflow using ${{ secrets.YOUR_SECRET_NAME }}, ensuring that sensitive data is not exposed during the CI/CD process.

Example:

```
- name: Login to Docker
  run: echo ${{ secrets.DOCKER_PASSWORD }} | docker
  login -u ${{ secrets.DOCKER_USERNAME }} --password-stdin
```

Leverage Caching to Reduce Build Times

Dependencies, for example, Maven or npm packages, can significantly accelerate build times in CI workflows. The GitHub Actions cache mechanism allows you to skip re-downloading dependencies with each job run. It will be faster and more efficient, especially for big projects.

Example:

```
- name: Cache Maven dependencies
  uses: actions/cache@v3
  with:
    path: ~/.m2
    key: ${{ runner.os }}-maven-${{ hashFiles('**/pom.xml') }}
    restore-keys: ${{ runner.os }}-maven
```

Run Security and Performance Tests As Part of the CI Process

Security scanning and performance testing should be part of the CI/CD pipeline to catch issues early. Tools such as Trivy for container vulnerabilities or JMeter for load testing keep your deployments secure and reliable. Automating these tests ensures you don't ship potentially vulnerable or underperforming code.

Example:

```
- name: Run Security Scan
  uses: aquasecurity/trivy-action@v0.2.1
  with:
    image-ref: 'my-java-app'
```

Summary

This chapter covers automating Java application deployment using Docker and GitHub Actions. It begins with an overview of GitHub Actions, explaining how workflows triggered by events like code pushes can automate tasks such as building, testing, and deploying code. The chapter then shows how to set up a CI pipeline for Java using Maven, including caching to speed up builds.

It also explains how to containerize a Java app using Docker and automate this process with GitHub Actions. Best practices include reusing workflows, securing sensitive data, optimizing Docker images with multi-stage builds, and running security tests. These steps streamline and secure the CI/CD process. This chapter also covers how we can deploy Docker images to GCP using GitHub Actions as the CI/CD process.

CHAPTER 8

Exploring Docker Alternatives

While Docker has been the go-to solution for containerization, the container ecosystem has evolved much, introducing a few powerful alternatives that address some of the pain points in modern development environments. This chapter goes through four of the most popular Docker alternatives, Podman, Buildah, Kaniko, and img, each of which offers unique advantages in different containerization needs. From Podman's daemonless architecture and improvements in security compared to Docker through Buildah-specific image building capability, to a CI/CD-optimized setup by Kaniko, and through img's easier container image construction, these applications represent the emerging wave of container solutions. Whether it's security, efficiency, or requirements of specific use cases, all these Docker alternatives are necessary for understanding how one should proceed during the journey toward containerization.

Podman

Podman is an open source software under which containers could be created, managed, and run on any Linux operating system, originally developed and maintained by Red Hat with functionality quite like Docker.

© Ashish Choudhary 2025
A. Choudhary, *When Docker Meets Java*, https://doi.org/10.1007/979-8-8688-1300-9_8

It has some distinct features:

- **Daemonless**: It is daemonless because it does not require having a central daemon as does Docker. A daemonless architecture enhances security and reduces overhead since every container will run separately under the identity of the user.

- **Rootless**: Podman runs containers without requiring root privileges, which is a huge security advantage over Docker. This reduces the likelihood of a security breach through the method of container escape (i.e., refers to a form of vulnerability by which the attacker breaks free from the container boundaries to gain access to the potential underlying operating system of the host).

- **Docker compatibility**: Podman is designed to be compatible with the CLI interface of Docker. Therefore, most of the Docker commands can be replaced by the podman command.

- **Pod concept**: Kubernetes introduced the concept of pods (i.e., groups of containers that can be treated collectively as a single unit). Podman uses similar concept, but it is suitable for single-node use cases and lacks the orchestration capabilities of Kubernetes.

These features make Podman a good alternative to Docker, especially when security and resource efficiency are considered.

Setting Up Podman

To install Podman Desktop on a Mac, you have two main methods: using the .dmg file or Homebrew. Here are the detailed steps for both methods:

Using homebrew: If you haven't already installed Homebrew (a package manager for macOS), you can install it by running the following command in your terminal:

```
$ /bin/bash -c "$(curl -fsSL https://raw.githubusercontent.com/
Homebrew/install/HEAD/install.sh)"
```

- Once Homebrew is installed, you can install Podman by running the following command in your terminal:

  ```
  $ brew install podman
  ```

- After installing Podman, you need to initialize a virtual machine (VM) which Podman will use to run containers. Do this by running:

  ```
  $ podman machine init
  ```

- To start the Podman VM, run:

  ```
  $ podman machine start
  ```

- Finally, you can verify that Podman is installed correctly by running:

  ```
  $ podman version
  ```

This command should display the installed version of Podman.

Using the .dmg File

- Go to the Podman Desktop website and download the .dmg file from the Downloads section. Choose the "universal" binary file or the one appropriate for your Mac's hardware architecture (Intel or Apple M1).

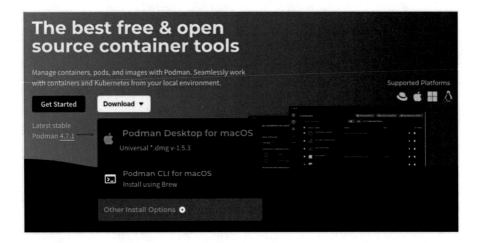

Figure 8-1. *Podman binary downloading*

- Locate the downloaded `.dmg` file, typically in the Downloads folder, and double-click to open it. Drag the Podman Desktop icon to the Applications folder.

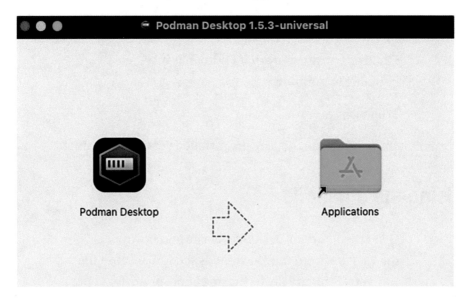

Figure 8-2. *Podman installation*

- Open Podman Desktop from the Launchpad or the
  Applications directory on your Mac.

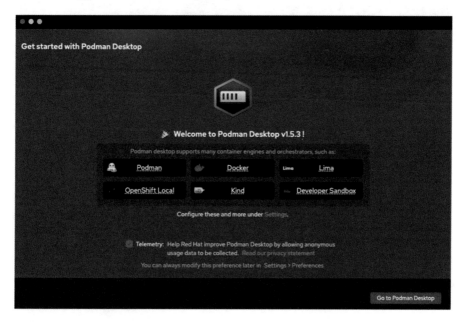

Figure 8-3. *Podman Desktop*

- When you open Podman Desktop for the first time,
  you'll be prompted to install it if Podman CLI/Engine
  is not found in the PATH. Click the "View detection
  checks" button and then the "Install" button to
  proceed.

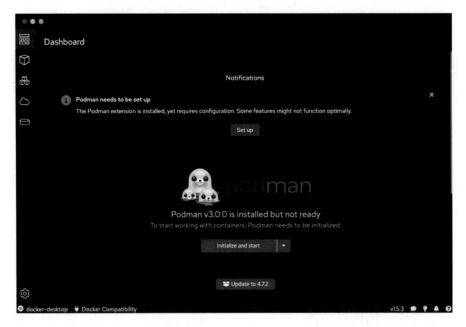

Figure 8-4. Podman dashboard

- You will be redirected to the Podman Installer. Follow the on-screen instructions.

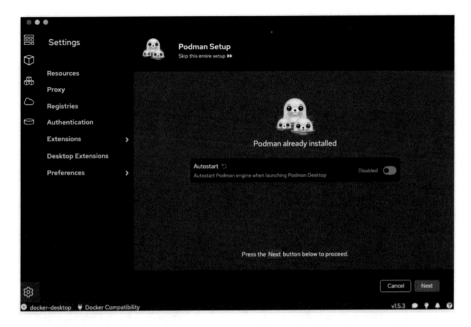

Figure 8-5. *Podman setup*

- Create podman machine.

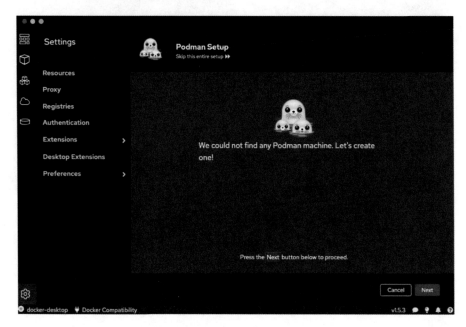

Figure 8-6. *Creating Podman machine*

- Set up required resources. Default options are good enough.

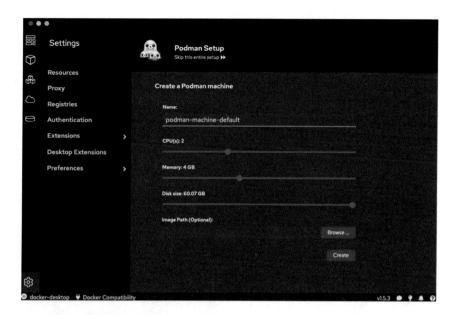

Figure 8-7. *Setting up resources*

- After installation, close the installation program.

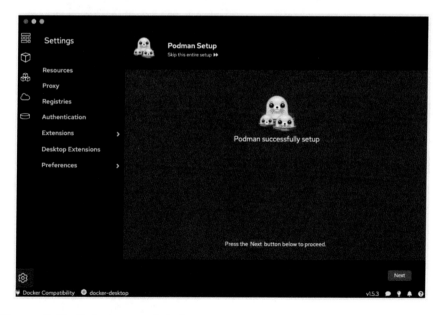

Figure 8-8. *Setup completed*

- The Podman Engine will be installed, and you are ready to use Podman Desktop.

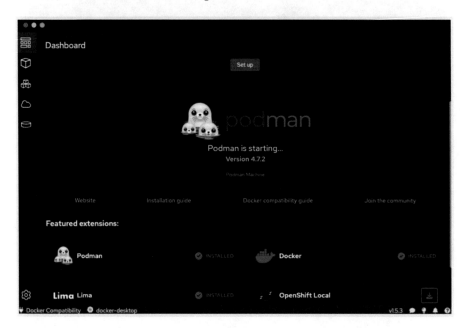

Figure 8-9. *Podman engine starting*

These steps will get Podman up and running on your Mac. Refer to the official Podman documentation or Mac-specific installation guides for detailed instructions or troubleshooting.

Developing a Simple Spring Boot Application

Visit Spring Initializr: Go to start.spring.io.

Project configuration: Select your project settings:

- Choose either Maven Project or Gradle Project.

- Select your preferred language (Java, Kotlin, or Groovy).

- Choose a Spring Boot version (usually, the default version is fine).

- Fill in the project metadata, like Group and Artifact.

Dependencies: Add the "Spring Web" dependency, which is essential for creating web applications.

Generate project: Click "Generate" to download your project zip file.

Open and run the project:

- Extract the downloaded zip file and open it in your favorite IDE (like IntelliJ IDEA, Eclipse, or VS Code).

- Find the `DemoApplication.java` file in the `src/main/java` directory under the package you specified.

- Write a simple REST controller or modify the existing `DemoApplication.java` to return a "Hello World" message upon visiting a specific URL.

Run the application:

- Execute the main method in the `DemoApplication.java` file to start the application.

- Once running, you can access the "Hello World" message by navigating to `localhost:8080` of your web browser.

This process creates a basic Spring Boot application that can be further developed or containerized.

Containerizing the Spring Boot Application

Now, containerize your application. Create a `Dockerfile` (or `Containerfile`) in the project root. This file instructs how to build your application's image. Include the base Java image, add your application's jar file, and specify the entry point. Here's a basic example:

```
# Use an official Java runtime as a parent image
FROM eclipse-temurin:17-jdk-jammy
# Set the working directory in the container
WORKDIR /app
# Copy the jar file into the container at /app
COPY target/demo-0.0.1-SNAPSHOT.jar /app/hello-world.jar
# Make port 8080 available to the world outside this container
EXPOSE 8080
# Run the jar file
ENTRYPOINT ["java","-jar","/app/hello-world.jar"]
```

Building Container Image with Podman

To create a container image using Podman Desktop, start by navigating to the Images section within Podman Desktop and then click the **Build an Image** button at the top-right corner, as shown in the following image.

Figure 8-10. *Building an image*

This action opens a menu where we can choose our location for `Containerfile`, typically found in the root directory of the demo folder. Once the `Containerfile` is selected, you can assign a name to the container image, such as "my-custom-image."

158

Next, click **Build** to observe the creation of each image layer.

Figure 8-11. *Configuring containerfile*

You can find the image in your local image registry.

Figure 8-12. *Image in local registry*

Running Containerized Application

Great! Now, head back to the Images section to view the containerized Spring Boot application, which has been successfully built and tagged as an image. To run this image as a container on our system, click the **Run** icon to the right of our container image, as shown in the following image.

Figure 8-13. *Run the image*

In the Port Mapping section, ensure that port 8080 of the container is mapped to port 8080 of the host. You can leave all other settings unchanged. Then, click **Start Container** to initiate the containerized version of your Spring Boot application, as illustrated in the following image.

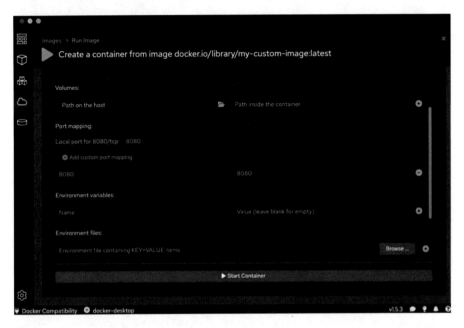

Figure 8-14. *Port mapping*

Now, the container is up and running.

Figure 8-15. *Container up and running*

We have now successfully built and containerized a Spring Boot application using Podman. This approach simplifies development and ensures our application is ready for deployment in any environment that supports containers.

Buildah

Buildah is an open source tool that provides a command-line interface for creating and managing OCI (Open Container Initiative) compliant container images. As an alternative to Docker, Buildah is part of the suite of tools provided by Red Hat, along with Podman and Skopeo, to work with containers.

Buildah is specialized in building container images. It doesn't manage container life cycle operations like starting, stopping, or orchestrating containers. Buildah does not include a container runtime; it creates and prepares images.

Buildah Features

Here are some critical aspects of Buildah:

Feature	Description
Rootless Container Image Building	Buildah can create container images without requiring any access privileges, reducing the risk of privilege escalation attacks.
Daemonless Architecture	Buildah operates without a central daemon, minimizing system resource usage and simplifying architecture by treating each operation as a separate process.
Compatibility with Dockerfiles	Buildah can build images from existing Dockerfiles, easing the transition for users familiar with Docker.
Flexibility in Image Building	Users can build images from scratch or using existing images, allowing for greater customization compared to Docker.
Integration with Other Tools	Buildah integrates well with other tools like Podman for running containers and Skopeo for transferring and inspecting images.
Fully Scriptable CLI	Buildah's CLI is fully scriptable, making it suitable for use in build and deployment pipelines.
OCI Images Support	Buildah generates images that are fully compatible with OCI-compliant tools and systems.

Podman and Buildah Comparison

Let's do a feature comparison between Podman and Buildah.

Feature	Buildah	Podman
Project Type	Open source	Open source
Platform	Available on Linux	Available on Linux
Primary Function	Building OCI images quickly, either with or without a Dockerfile	Managing OCI images and containers, including pulling, tagging, creating, and running containers
Dockerfile Support	Can build images from a Dockerfile or without one	Supports Docker commands, designed as a drop-in replacement for Docker
Daemon Dependency	Does not run as a daemon	Does not run as a daemon
Root Privileges	Operates without root privileges	Operates without root privileges
Container Lifecycle	Typically short-lived containers for building images	Supports long-lived traditional containers
Storage Systems	Uses a different storage system from Podman	Uses a different storage system from Buildah
Integration	Complements Podman in building images	Complements Buildah by managing containers

Figure 8-16. *Podman and Buildah match made in heaven*

Building Images with Buildah

To start with Buildah, you can install it on any Linux distribution supporting OCI. Here's a quick guide:

Installation

On Fedora/Linux/CentOS, you can install Buildah with `sudo dnf install buildah`.

On Ubuntu, first, add the Kubic project's repository with `sudo add-apt-repository ppa:projectatomic/ppa` followed by `sudo apt-get update` and then `sudo apt-get install buildah`.

Building an image: To create a new image, you can start with a base image or from scratch, then use the Buildah commands to modify the filesystem, set up the environment variables, expose ports, and define entry points.

Committing your work: Once done with the changes, you can commit the working container to an image using `buildah commit`.

Pushing to a registry: Finally, you can push your image to a container registry with `buildah push`.

Let's say you want to create a simple container image with a web server:

```
# Create a new container from scratch
new_container=$(buildah from scratch)
# Mount the container filesystem
mountpoint=$(buildah mount $new_container)
# Install a web server, for example, nginx
dnf install --installroot $mountpoint --releasever
30 nginx --setopt install_weak_deps=false -y
# Set up some configurations and static HTML files
echo 'Hello from Buildah!' > $mountpoint/usr/share/nginx/html/
index.html
# Commit the changes to create a new image
buildah commit $new_container my-webserver
# Push the image to a registry
buildah push my-webserver docker://myregistry/my-
webserver:latest
```

Buildah focuses on building container images, whereas Docker provides a broader range of features, including orchestration and networking. For users primarily focused on building and managing container images, especially in a more scriptable and flexible manner, Buildah offers a robust alternative to Docker's image-building capabilities.

Kaniko

Docker has become synonymous with creating and managing containers in containerization. However, building Docker images typically requires a Docker daemon, which poses challenges in environments where running a daemon isn't feasible or secure. This is where Kaniko enters the picture, offering a solution to build container images in environments like continuous integration (CI) pipelines without needing a Docker daemon.

Need for Kaniko

Kaniko was developed by Google to address specific challenges in building Docker images:

- **Security concerns**: Running a Docker daemon typically requires elevated privileges, which can pose security risks, especially in shared CI environments.

- **Environment limitations**: Running a Docker daemon isn't practical in specific environments, like Kubernetes clusters.

- **Efficiency in ci/cd pipelines**: Kaniko optimizes building images directly within a CI/CD pipeline without relying on a separate environment to run Docker.

Features of Kaniko

Kaniko boasts several features that make it advantageous for building Docker images:

- **No daemon required**: Kaniko doesn't need a Docker daemon to build an image, reducing the attack surface and making it safer in shared environments.

- **Works in userspace**: It executes each command in a Dockerfile entirely in userspace, making it compatible with various environments.

- **Caching mechanisms**: Kaniko provides caching options to speed up consecutive builds.

- **Supports standard dockerfile directives**: You can use the same Dockerfile you would with Docker, making it easy to integrate into existing workflows.

Understanding Kaniko

The Kaniko executor image (i.e., gcr.io/kaniko-project/executor:latest) builds an image from a Dockerfile and pushes it to a registry. It begins by extracting the filesystem from the base image specified by the FROM command in the Dockerfile. The executor then runs the Dockerfile commands, taking a snapshot of the filesystem in userspace after each execution. If any changes occur, it appends a new layer of these files to the base image and updates the image metadata accordingly.

Using Kaniko to Build and Push Docker Images

- **Step 1: Preparing your Dockerfile and context:**
  First, prepare your Dockerfile as usual. Ensure all files referenced in the Dockerfile are available in the build context.

- **Step 2: Setting up Docker Registry credentials:**
  Kaniko needs access to your registry to push the built image. You'll need to create a JSON file with your credentials. This file typically looks like this:

```json
{
  "auths": {
    "https://index.docker.io/v1/": {
      "username": "yourusername",
      "password": "yourpassword"
    }
  }
}
```

- **Step 3: Running Kaniko in Docker:** You don't need Kubernetes to run Kaniko. It can be executed as a Docker container. Here's how:

  1. **Mount your context and credential**: Use Docker to run Kaniko, mounting the build context directory and the directory containing your Docker registry credentials.

     ```
     docker run --rm \
       -v $(pwd):/workspace \
       -v /path/to/kaniko/.docker/:/kaniko/.docker/ \
       gcr.io/kaniko-project/executor:latest \
       --dockerfile /workspace/Dockerfile \
       --context dir:///workspace/ \
       --destination yourdockerhubusername/your-image-
     name:your-tag
     ```

  2. **Build and push**: Kaniko will build the image using the provided Dockerfile and context and then push it to the specified destination in your Docker registry.

- **Step 4: Verifying the image:** After the build process, verify the image in your Docker registry to ensure it's been correctly pushed.

Kaniko is mainly for rootless, daemonless, and secure image building in environments that might not be suitable for Docker, such as in CI/CD or Kubernetes environments. With Kaniko, developers and DevOps teams can securely and efficiently streamline their CI/CD workflows.

Img

In the evolving landscape of containerization, the need for versatile, secure, and easy-to-use tools for building container images has never been greater. This is where img comes into play, offering a fresh approach to image creation in Docker and container technology.

Why img?

img was developed to address several challenges and limitations posed by traditional Docker image building methods:

Daemonless operation: The build process of a Docker image requires the daemon. This may pose a security problem—mainly in shared or multitenant environments, CI systems.

Root privileges: Docker requires root privilege to create the images, which is a great concern in terms of security, of course. img does not require any root access.

Simplicity and portability: img is a tool which supports building, pushing, and pulling images easily, and, therefore, becomes rather attractive to developers and pipelines for CI/CD.

Features of img

img stands out with its distinct features:

Unprivileged and daemonless: img runs totally in userspace and does not require any daemon, so it enhances security as well as reduces the attack surface.

Compatibility with Docker and OCI images: It can build images from Dockerfiles compatible with Docker and other OCI image formats.

Efficient caching: Thanks to its efficient caching mechanism, all repeated builds are faster via img.

Easy integration into CI/CD pipelines: It is very simple and does not require privileged requirements, so it quite easily fits into automated workflows.

Using img to Build and Push Docker Images

Step 1. Installing img: First, install img on your system. It's available for various platforms and can be downloaded from its GitHub repository.

Step 2. Preparing your Dockerfile: Ensure your Dockerfile is ready with all necessary instructions for building your image.

Step 3. Building the image with img: Navigate to the directory containing your Dockerfile and run:

```
$ img build -t yourusername/yourimagename:tag .
```

Replace `yourusername/yourimagename:tag` with your Docker Hub username, image name, and tag. `img` will build the image based on your Dockerfile.

Step 4. Pushing the image to a registry: Before pushing the image, authenticate with your Docker registry:

```
$ img login -u yourusername -p yourpassword
```

Then, push the image to Docker Hub or another registry:

```
$ img push yourusername/yourimagename:tag
```

Step 5. Verifying the image: After pushing, check your Docker registry to ensure the image has been uploaded successfully.

`img` emerges as a very powerful tool for building Docker and OCI images, especially suited for environments where security, simplicity, and integration with the existing pipelines are paramount. This allows unprivileged, daemonless image creation, which solves key challenges in the container ecosystem. It is a valuable asset for developers and DevOps professionals because its adoption can streamline workflows, enhance security, and efficiently manage container images.

Summary

This chapter presents four alternatives of Docker and points out what each is useful for in the container ecosystems:

Podman is a standalone alternative for Docker. It supports daemonless architecture combined with rootless container management. Podman supports all native Docker commands but adds another feature: pod management. This chapter deals with the installation of Podman in Mac systems and then demonstrates it in practice by containerizing a Spring Boot application.

Buildah is focused on creating container images, giving developers more flexibility and control of the image-building process. It does not require any root privileges and integrates well with other container tools. This chapter explores some of the features of Buildah and provides practical examples of building container images from scratch.

Kaniko solves the problem of constructing Docker images in restricted environments where it is not feasible, especially within CI/CD pipeline runs. It operates completely without a Docker daemon. It is designed to run inside a container. Furthermore, the entire build process occurs entirely in user space, which makes it perfectly legal to use when an image has to be built in extremely constrained environments. It has been specifically optimized for Kubernetes and cloud-native workflows.

img is a contemporary approach to creating container images, which is based on simplicity and security. It runs in userspace and does not require root privilege or daemon, so it is really very well suited for the CI/CD environment. The chapter ends with practical advice on using img to build and manage your container images.

Together, these tools demonstrate the diverse approaches available for container management beyond Docker, each offering unique advantages for specific use cases and environments. Understanding these alternatives helps developers and organizations choose the most appropriate tools for their containerization needs.

CHAPTER 9

Building Native Images with GraalVM

Learn about building lightning-fast cloud Java applications with GraalVM and Quarkus.

In a cloud-native world, the facility to convert Java applications into efficient, lightweight executables has gained much importance. Docker containers revolutionized application packaging and deployment but still carry the overhead of running a full JVM inside each container, increasing memory usage and slowing down startups. This is where GraalVM shines as it overcomes these limitations by converting Java bytecode into standalone native executables that start almost instantly and consume significantly less memory—features especially valuable in microservices architectures and serverless environments.

Furthermore, you will learn about: GraalVM Native Images, GraalVM native image support in Spring Boot 3, and the Quarkus framework—all unique in their approach to optimizing Java applications for modern deployment environments.

© Ashish Choudhary 2025
A. Choudhary, *When Docker Meets Java*, https://doi.org/10.1007/979-8-8688-1300-9_9

Demystifying Native Image and GraalVM

GraalVM is an Oracle Labs-developed, high-performance, polyglot virtual machine designed to enable multiple programming languages to be executed on a single runtime. It was made to make improvements in performance while reducing the overhead of conventional JVM-based execution.

A native image in the context of Java and GraalVM refers to a standalone executable file created from Java bytecode. Before we go deeper, let's understand this with a restaurant and kitchen analogy:

- **Traditional JVM**: A fully equipped kitchen with various appliances and tools. It can cook any dish but takes time to prepare and clean.

- **Native image**: A food truck tailored to a specific cuisine type. It's smaller, starts cooking faster, and is more efficient, but can't change its menu easily.

Native Image Explained

- **Conversion**: Transforms Java bytecode into a platform-specific executable.

- **Components**: Includes the application classes, dependencies, and statically linked native code from JDK.

- **No JVM required**: The JVM is packaged into the executable, eliminating the need for a Java Runtime Environment on the target system.

Figure 9-1. *Native image creation steps*

Native Image Benefits

Benefit	Description
Instant Startup	Native images start faster than traditional JVM-based applications.
Reduced Memory Footprint	Consumes less memory, enhancing performance, especially in constrained environments like containers or serverless.
Lightweight Deployment	Ideal for cloud-native applications due to smaller size and compatibility with containerization.

Native Image Drawbacks

Drawback	Description
Platform Dependency	Each native image is specific to a platform, requiring multiple builds for cross-platform compatibility.
Limited Java Features	Some dynamic features of Java, like reflection, may not be fully supported or require additional configuration.
Complex Debugging	Debugging native images can be more challenging than traditional Java applications.

Differences Between Docker and Native Image

Native images and Docker images serve different purposes and operate at different levels in the software deployment process:

Term	Scope	Purpose	Use Case
Native Image	Specific to a compiled executable from Java code using tools like GraalVM.	Create a platform-specific, standalone executable with necessary Java classes and a reduced JVM.	Optimizes Java applications for faster startup and lower memory footprint.
Docker Image	A lightweight, standalone, executable package that includes everything needed to run software, including code, runtime, system tools, libraries, and settings.	Ensures consistent environments and portability across different systems.	Used for containerizing applications to run them in isolated environments.

A native image focuses on optimizing a specific Java application, while a Docker image is about packaging and running software consistently in various environments. A native image can be part of a Docker image, but they are fundamentally different in their core functionalities and objectives.

Understanding GraalVM

GraalVM is a high-performance polyglot virtual machine developed by Oracle. It enhances the capabilities of the standard Java Virtual Machine (JVM) by offering the following features:

1. **Support for multiple languages**: Apart from Java,
   it can run applications written in JavaScript, Ruby,
   Python, and other JVM languages.

2. **Just-in-time compiler (JIT)**: Improves the
   performance of Java applications by compiling
   bytecode to machine code at runtime.

3. **Ahead-of-time compiler (AOT)**: Through
   the Native Image technology, it compiles Java
   applications into standalone executables, which
   start faster and require less memory.

4. **Interoperability**: Enables seamless integration
   between different programming languages.

5. **Extension and customization**: Developers
   can extend and customize the VM for specific
   requirements.

JIT vs. AOT Compiler

Feature	JIT	AOT
Timing	Compiles code during runtime.	Compiles code before runtime, during the build process.
Operation	Translates bytecode into machine code when a program is running.	Produces a binary executable specific to a platform.
Performance	Optimizes code based on runtime data, potentially achieving high performance.	Faster startup times as code is pre-compiled, but lacks runtime optimization.

(continued)

Feature	JIT	AOT
Flexibility	More adaptable since it compiles code as needed.	Less flexible, as it's compiled for specific architectures or platforms.
Memory usage	Can increase memory usage and startup time due to runtime compilation.	Generally has a smaller memory footprint and reduces runtime overhead.

JVM vs. GraalVM

Feature	JVM	GraalVM
Language support	Primarily supports Java and JVM-based languages like Scala or Kotlin.	Supports additional languages like JavaScript, Ruby, Python, and R, making it a polyglot VM.
Performance optimization	Uses just-in-time (JIT) compilation to optimize bytecode at runtime.	Includes an advanced JIT compiler (Graal Compiler) for more efficient performance optimizations.
Ahead-Of-Time compilation	Doesn't natively support AOT compilation.	Offers Native Image technology for AOT compilation, creating standalone executables from Java applications.
Interoperability	Limited to JVM-based language interoperability.	Enhanced interoperability features, allowing for mixed-language applications.

(continued)

Feature	JVM	GraalVM
Code elimination	No exclusion of unreachable code from final executable.	Unreachable code at the time of native image creation is excluded from the final executable.
Immutable classpath	In traditional JVM applications, the classpath can be modified dynamically, allowing the addition or modification of where the JVM searches for classes and resources.	The classpath is fixed at the time of building and cannot be altered.
Dynamic code awareness	JVM has ability to adapt to dynamic code changes, including loading classes that were unknown at compile time, is one of its core strengths, allowing for flexible and dynamic Java applications.	GraalVM requires explicit instructions about dynamic code aspects such as reflection, resources, serialization, and dynamic proxies.

GraalVM's ability to support multiple languages and improve application performance makes it a versatile tool for modern software development.

Spring Boot 3 and GraalVM

GraalVM is a version of OpenJDK enhanced with additional features, including the "native-image" utility. This utility performs ahead-of-time (AOT) compilation, efficiently processing your code to eliminate unneeded parts and then converting the remainder into highly optimized, system-specific native code. The performance improvements are remarkable, akin to those seen in C or Go applications. It results in binaries that start almost instantly and require significantly less RAM. With this technology, deploying a Spring Boot application can consume tens of megabytes of RAM and start in just a few hundred milliseconds.

To leverage this, use `./gradlew nativeCompile` or `./mvnw -Pnative native:compile`. Both commands are used when creating native images in the context of GraalVM—a virtual machine that enables just-in-time (JIT) compilation of Java applications to platform-dependent executables, thus reducing startup time and memory usage.

Spring Boot has officially supported this feature for production use since the release of Spring Boot 3.0 in November 2022.

Building Native Images with Spring Boot

To initiate a new native Spring Boot project with ease, navigate to start. spring.io , select the **GraalVM Native Support** dependency, and proceed to generate your project.

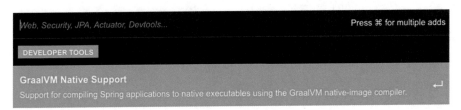

Figure 9-2. *Adding GraalVM dependency*

There are two main ways to build a Spring Boot native image application, and they are:

Using Spring Boot support for cloud-native buildpacks: This method generates a lightweight container containing a native executable.

This method is the most straightforward starting point for those familiar with Spring Boot's container image support.

Note   Docker installation on the target machine is required.

With Maven to create the image, run the following goal:

```
$ mvn -Pnative spring-boot:build-image
```

With Gradle to create the image, run the following goal:

```
$ gradle bootBuildImage
```

Then, you can run the app like any other container:

```
$ docker run --rm demo:0.0.1-SNAPSHOT
```

Using GraalVM native build tools: This approach generates a native executable directly. Opt for this choice if you're interested in broader capabilities, such as conducting tests within a native image environment. It's essential to have the GraalVM native-image compiler installed and ready on your system for this option.

Note   GraalVM 22.3+ is required.

With Maven to create the executable, run the following goal:

```
$ mvn -Pnative native:compile
```

With Gradle to create the executable, run the following goal:

```
$ gradle nativeCompile
```

For executing a Maven-built native image, use this command:

```
$ target/demo
```

For executing a Gradle-built native image, use this command:

```
$ build/native/nativeCompile/myproject
```

These methods offer different advantages and can be chosen based on the specific needs and environment of the application.

Here is a diagram explaining the build process using both methods for building native images with Spring Boot.

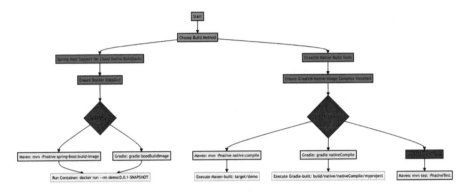

Figure 9-3. *Spring Boot GraalVM build process*

Testing GraalVM Native Image for Spring Boot Application

In the realm of GraalVM native image applications, it's recommended to run most unit and integration tests on the JVM for efficiency and seamless IDE integration. Testing focuses on ensuring the Spring AOT engine processes the application correctly and GraalVM can produce a valid native image. Developers can test AOT processing using the JVM by enabling the spring.aot.enabled property.

```
$ java -Dspring.aot.enabled=true -jar myapplication.jar
```

Additionally, Spring Framework supports running tests in a native image environment, a feature particularly useful in CI pipelines. This approach requires setting up specific Maven or Gradle configurations and using relevant build tools.

When setting up Maven for running native tests, make sure your `pom.xml` file is configured with `spring-boot-starter-parent` as the parent. This requires including a `<parent>` section in your `pom.xml` that aligns with this specification.

```
<parent>
    <groupId>org.springframework.boot</groupId>
    <artifactId>spring-boot-starter-parent</artifactId>
    <version>3.2.0</version>
</parent>
```

You can also run your existing test suite in a native image. This is an efficient way to validate the compatibility of your application.

To run your existing tests in a native image, run the following goal:

```
$ mvn test -PnativeTest
```

When using the Spring Boot Gradle plugin along with the GraalVM Native Image plugin, AOT test tasks are set up automatically. It's important to ensure your Gradle build script includes a `plugins` block that contains `org.graalvm.buildtools.native`.

For executing native tests using Gradle, you should utilize the `nativeTest` task.

```
$ gradle nativeTest
```

Understanding Quarkus a Kubernetes Native Java Framework

In the ever-evolving world of software development, efficiency and speed are paramount. Quarkus, a Kubernetes-native Java framework, is revolutionizing the way Java applications are developed and deployed in cloud environments. This section will introduce you to the basics of Quarkus and why it's becoming a game-changer for Java developers.

Knowing Quarkus

Quarkus is an open source Java framework designed for Kubernetes, the widely used container orchestration platform. It optimizes Java specifically for containers, enabling it to become an effective platform for serverless, cloud, and Kubernetes environments.

Key Features of Quarkus

- **Container first**: Quarkus is built with container-based environments in mind, ensuring low memory footprint and fast startup times.

- **Imperative and reactive**: It seamlessly supports both imperative and reactive programming models, catering to a wide range of application architectures.

- **Microservices ready**: With built-in support for microservices patterns, Quarkus is ideal for building scalable and maintainable applications.

- **Developer joy**: Offers live coding, unified configuration, and streamlined code for both imperative and reactive coding.

Need for Quarkus with Kubernetes

- **Fast startup and low memory footprint**: Quarkus applications start in milliseconds and consume a fraction of the memory compared to traditional Java applications. This is crucial for Kubernetes, where resources are scaled up and down frequently.

- **Developer productivity**: Quarkus enhances developer productivity with hot-reload capabilities, meaning you can see changes in real time without restarting your application.

- **Native compilation with GraalVM**: Quarkus can be compiled into a native executable using GraalVM, further reducing the memory footprint and startup time.

- **Cloud-native ecosystem integration**: It integrates smoothly with Kubernetes, Docker, and cloud-native databases and messaging systems.

Getting Started with Quarkus

The easiest way to get started with Quarkus is to use `code.quarkus.io` which is an online platform provided by the Quarkus team that significantly simplifies the process of creating a new Quarkus project. It's designed to be user-friendly and efficient, especially helpful for beginners or those looking to quickly bootstrap a new Quarkus-based application.

Here's an overview of what `code.quarkus.io` offers:

- **User-friendly interface**: The website has an intuitive interface that makes it easy to create and configure a Quarkus project without writing any boilerplate code.

- **Customizable project setup**: You can customize various aspects of your project, such as the Maven Group, Artifact, and Version. You can also choose the build tool (Maven or Gradle).

- **Extensions selection**: One of the most powerful features code.quarkus.io offered is the ability to browse and select from a wide range of Quarkus extensions. Extensions are add-ons or libraries that integrate with Quarkus to provide additional functionality, like database connectivity, security, messaging, and more.

- **Streamlined dependencies management**: It automatically manages dependencies for the selected extensions, ensuring compatibility and reducing the hassle of manual dependency management.

- **Download or share your project**: After configuring your project, you can either download it as a ZIP file or share it with others using a generated URL. This feature is particularly useful for collaboration or for saving project configurations for future use.

- **Code generation**: The platform generates some basic code and configuration files based on your selections, helping you jump-start development.

Steps to create your first project.

- **Access the platform**: Visit code.quarkus.io in your web browser.

- **Configure your project**: Input your project's groupId, artifactId, and version. Select your preferred build tool.

- **Select extensions**: Browse through the list of available extensions. You can search for specific extensions or filter them by category.

- **Generate your project**: Once you've made your selections, click on the "Generate your application" button. This will create a customized Quarkus project.

- **Download/share**: You can then download the generated project as a ZIP file or copy the URL to share with others.

- **Start coding**: Unzip the downloaded file and open it in your favorite IDE or editor to start coding.

Figure 9-4. *Quarkus project onboarding*

Quarkus marks a significant shift in the Java ecosystem, bringing Java squarely into the modern cloud-native era. It's not just about running Java in Kubernetes; it's about making Java a first-class citizen in this landscape. With its unparalleled efficiency and developer-focused design, Quarkus is undoubtedly a framework worth exploring for any Java developer looking to step into the world of Kubernetes and cloud-native development.

Building and Deploying Quarkus Application on Kubernetes

In the world of cloud-native development, Kubernetes has emerged as the de facto standard for orchestrating containerized applications. Quarkus, known as "Supersonic Subatomic Java," is a Kubernetes-native Java framework tailored for GraalVM and HotSpot. This section will guide you through the process of building and deploying a Quarkus application on Kubernetes.

Up and Running with Quarkus

Step 1: We can start by generating a new Quarkus project. We can use code.quarkus.io to set up the project with the desired extensions, or use Maven/Gradle directly:

```
mvn io.quarkus.platform:quarkus-maven-plugin:3.6.4:create \
    -DprojectGroupId=org.acme \
    -DprojectArtifactId=kubernetes-quickstart \
    -Dextensions='resteasy-reactive,kubernetes,jib'
cd kubernetes-quickstart
```

This will create a new project containing the Kubernetes and Jib extensions. Furthermore, the following dependencies are added to our pom.xml file.

```
<dependency>
    <groupId>io.quarkus</groupId>
    <artifactId>quarkus-resteasy-reactive</artifactId>
</dependency>
```

```
<dependency>
    <groupId>io.quarkus</groupId>
    <artifactId>quarkus-kubernetes</artifactId>
</dependency>
<dependency>
    <groupId>io.quarkus</groupId>
    <artifactId>quarkus-container-image-jib</artifactId>
</dependency>
```

By incorporating these dependencies, we facilitate the automatic creation of Kubernetes manifests with each build and simultaneously enable container image building using Jib. For instance, after executing the following:

```
./mvnw install
```

Among the various generated files, we will observe two specific files—kubernetes.json and kubernetes.yml—located in the target/ kubernetes/ directory. When examining either of these files, it becomes apparent that they include definitions for a Kubernetes Deployment as well as a Service.

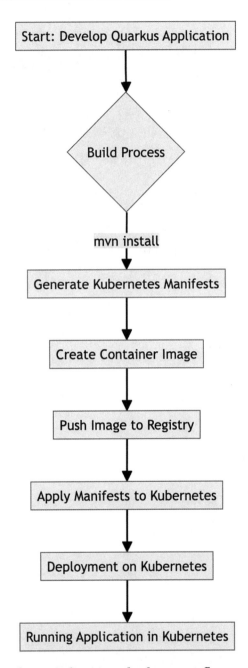

Figure 9-5. *Quarkus application deployment flow*

Just to reiterate, Quarkus offers the ability to automatically generate Kubernetes resources based on sane defaults and user-supplied configuration using dekorate .

Furthermore, Quarkus can deploy the application to a target Kubernetes cluster by applying the generated manifests to the target cluster's API Server.

```
kubectl apply -f target/kubernetes/kubernetes.json
```

Finally, when either one of the container image extensions is present, Quarkus can create a container image and push it to a registry before deploying the application to the target platform.

Summary

The chapter gave a detailed overview of how to build native images with GraalVM and integrate them with popular frameworks like Spring Boot. Although GraalVM native images have significant advantages, such as faster startup times and lower memory footprint, some limitations limit support of Java's dynamic features such as reflection.

Then, the discussion moves on to Spring Boot 3 native support which offers two main ways of building native images: Cloud Native Buildpacks and GraalVM Native Build Tools.

Last but not least, it covers Quarkus, a Kubernetes-native Java framework built from the ground up for container environments, focusing on its features like live coding and support for imperative and reactive programming. Throughout the chapter, the focus remains on how these technologies are transforming Java applications to meet the demands of modern cloud-native architectures, particularly in containerized and Kubernetes.

CHAPTER 10

Testing Java Applications Using Testcontainers

Explore the practical approach to building production-like test environments for Dockerized applications using Testcontainers

In a moving landscape of software development, comprehensive testing is very critical to the reliability and robustness of any application. While unit testing gives insight into individual components, integration testing poses some unique challenges, especially when it comes to dependencies such as databases and services.

Testcontainers is a strong solution to these challenges, offering a Java library that leverages Docker containers to create lightweight, disposable instances of databases, web browsers, and other services essential for integration testing. This chapter shows how Testcontainers simplifies the testing process—specifically, Spring Boot applications—by providing a consistent, isolated testing environment that closely mimics production scenarios.

© Ashish Choudhary 2025
A. Choudhary, *When Docker Meets Java*, https://doi.org/10.1007/979-8-8688-1300-9_10

Introduction to Testcontainers

In software development, integration testing is crucial in ensuring that different parts of an application work together seamlessly. This is where Testcontainers, a Java library, steps in. Testcontainers provides lightweight, throwaway instances of common databases, Selenium web browsers, or anything else that can run in a Docker container.

The library is designed to support our automated integration tests, providing a higher level of confidence before moving to production. Using Docker containers, Testcontainers ensure that the application behaves as expected in an environment that closely mimics production.

Need for Testcontainers

Testcontainers is an open source framework for providing throwaway, lightweight instances of databases, message brokers, web browsers, or anything that can run in a Docker container.

Think of Testcontainers as a toy box for our computer programs. When we are playing with toy blocks, we might want to see how they all fit together to create a toy bridge. But we can't complete our toy bridge without missing blocks. Testcontainers allow our program to borrow any blocks we might be missing, like a unique block, so we can see if our creation works with those pieces too. Like we would test if our toy bridge holds up when cars drive over it, Testcontainers lets our program check if it works well with real pieces, not just pretend ones. And for programs written with Spring Boot, it's like getting the best toy blocks that fit perfectly right out of the box.

With Testcontainers, integration testing becomes more realistic. It allows us to conduct tests using the real versions of our application's databases and services, following the true behaviors our code is supposed to perform, instead of using stand-ins that might oversimplify or skip over important details.

194

Figure 10-1. *Testcontainers logo*

Testcontainers are needed for several reasons in the context of integration testing:

- **Environment parity**: It provides a way to run tests against real services and databases, ensuring that the test environment closely mirrors production.

- **Ease of use**: Testcontainers manage the life cycle of containers used in testing, simplifying the setup and teardown process.

- **Portability**: Tests using Testcontainers can be run on any system where Docker is available without additional service configuration.

- **Continuous integration (CI) friendly**: Testcontainers are ideal for CI pipelines as they allow tests to run in isolation and in a repeatable manner.

- **Flexibility**: Developers can quickly test against different database and service versions by changing container versions.

- **Resource efficiency**: Containers can be started and stopped quickly on-demand, which is more efficient than managing dedicated test databases and services.

Testcontainers Features

These features make Testcontainers a powerful ally for developers looking to ensure their applications will work as expected when deployed in a real-world environment:

- **Diverse container support**: Offers lightweight, throwaway instances for various services, including databases, web browsers, and message brokers.

- **JUnit integration**: Seamlessly integrates with JUnit test cases.

- **Singleton containers**: Supports singleton containers that can be shared across multiple test classes.

- **Custom containers**: Allows the use of custom Docker images.

- **Database integration**: Direct support for popular databases with preconfigured JDBC URLs.

- **Mocking external services**: Facilitates testing applications that interact with third-party services by mocking those services in Docker containers.

- **Environment replication**: Provides a consistent environment replicating production settings, reducing "works on my machine" problems.

- **Resource management**: Handles the starting and stopping of containers, ensuring no wasted resources.

- **Service health checking**: Waits for containers to become healthy before proceeding with the tests.

- **Reusable containers**: Optimizes test runs by reusing containers between test runs when possible.

- **Log collection**: Allows collection and observation of container logs, which is helpful for debugging.

- **Life cycle control**: Gives developers control over container life cycle events within the test code.

Testing Spring Boot Applications

Unit and integration testing in Spring Boot applications guarantee the quality and reliability of the software. Focusing on individual components, unit testing enables early bug detection, which makes a huge difference in reducing rectification costs and complexity during later development stages. Such tests also act as documentation, showing how to use the code. This will even provide a safety net during refactoring, guaranteeing that updates or changes don't break existing functionality.

Integration testing, on the other hand, is necessary for ensuring that different components interact perfectly, thereby guaranteeing a cohesive working system. This also includes simulating the different environments, such as databases and web servers, to ensure the application performs well in real-world conditions. Unit and integration testing thus go a long way in ensuring the maintainability, robustness, and general reliability of Spring Boot applications.

Testing Spring Boot applications typically involves several layers of testing:

- **Unit testing**: Testing individual components in isolation using frameworks like JUnit and Mockito. Spring Boot's `@SpringBootTest` annotation can be used for more integration-style unit tests where Spring context is loaded.

- **Integration testing**: Testing the interaction between different layers of the application. This can involve using @DataJpaTest for repository layers, @WebMvcTest for controllers, and @SpringBootTest with TestRestTemplate or MockMvc for full context loading.

- **End-to-end testing**: Testing the entire application, often with @SpringBootTest to run the application and tools like Selenium for web UI testing.

- **Testcontainers**: For integration tests that require real services like databases or message brokers, Testcontainers provide a way to run these services in Docker containers during testing.

Each testing layer serves a different purpose, from quick unit tests to thorough end-to-end tests, ensuring that your Spring Boot application is robust and ready for production.

Unit Testing of Spring Boot Application

Let's say we have a simple EmployeeService class that we want to test:

```
import org.springframework.beans.factory.annotation.Autowired;
import org.springframework.stereotype.Service;
@Service
public class EmployeeService {
    private final EmployeeRepository employeeRepository;
    @Autowired
    public EmployeeService(EmployeeRepository
    employeeRepository) {
        this.employeeRepository = employeeRepository;
    }
```

```
public Employee addEmployee(Employee employee) {
    return employeeRepository.save(employee);
}
}
```

The addEmployee method is a simple example that adds a new employee to the repository. We can expand this class with additional methods to handle other CRUD operations.

This EmployeeService class relies on EmployeeRepository to handle data operations.

```
import org.springframework.data.repository.CrudRepository;
import org.springframework.stereotype.Repository;
@Repository
public interface EmployeeRepository extends
CrudRepository<Employee, Long> {
}
```

This repository interface provides basic CRUD operations for your Employee entity. You can extend it with custom query methods as needed.

In the following example, Employee is your entity class, and Long is the type of the entity's primary key. Here @RedisHash("Employee") annotation indicates that instances of Employee entity will be stored in Redis. The @Id annotation marks the field to be used as the identifier in Redis. The name and position fields are simple properties of the Employee entity.

```
import org.springframework.data.annotation.Id;
import org.springframework.data.redis.core.RedisHash;
@RedisHash("Employee")
public record Employee(@Id Long id, String name, String
position) {}
```

Java records automatically generate getters, equals(), hashCode(), and toString() methods, making them a perfect fit for simple data carrier classes like entities. Note that records are immutable, so every field is final.

In the following unit test, we are trying to mock the interaction with EmployeeRepository. Here's how you might write a unit test for EmployeeService using JUnit and Mockito:

Mockito is a popular Java testing framework that allows the creation of mock objects, simulating and verifying method invocations in unit tests.

```java
public class EmployeeServiceTest {
    private EmployeeService employeeService;
    private EmployeeRepository mockRepository;
    @BeforeEach
    void setUp() {
        mockRepository = Mockito.
        mock(EmployeeRepository.class);
        employeeService = new EmployeeService(mockRepository);
    }
    @Test
    void testAddEmployee() {
        Employee employee = new Employee("John Doe",
        "Developer");
        Mockito.when(mockRepository.save(employee)).
        thenReturn(employee);
        Employee result = employeeService.
        addEmployee(employee);
        assertEquals(employee.getName(), result.getName());
    }
}
```

Integration Testing of Spring Boot Application

Now, let's consider a scenario where we want to test an EmployeeRepository that interacts with a Redis database, but without using Testcontainers. This typically involves more manual setup and can be complex.

First, you'll need a running instance of Redis. This could be on your local machine, a Docker container started manually, or a managed service. Assuming we have a Redis instance running on localhost at the default port 6379, here's how the test might look:

```
@SpringBootTest
public class EmployeeRepositoryIntegrationTest {
    @Autowired
    private EmployeeRepository employeeRepository;
    @Test
    public void testEmployeeRepository() {
        Employee employee = new Employee("John Doe",
        "Developer");
        employeeRepository.save(employee);
        Optional<Employee> employee = employeeRepository.
        findById(employee.getId());
        assertTrue(employee.isPresent());
        assertEquals(employee.getName(), employee.get().
        getName());
    }
}
application-test.properties:
spring.redis.host=localhost
spring.redis.port=6379
```

The `application-test.properties` file in a Spring Boot application is used to define properties specifically for testing environments. When you run tests, Spring Boot can be configured to use these properties instead of the regular `application.properties` or `application.yml`. This allows for setting up different configurations for testing, such as connecting to a different database or using different application settings.

Adopting this manual approach to integration testing will introduce several complexities:

- This integration test assumes Redis is already running and accessible.

- We need to manually ensure that Redis is in a clean state before and after tests.

- Handling different environments (CI server, local development) can be challenging without Testcontainers.

- This approach lacks the isolation and environment parity provided by Testcontainers, potentially leading to flaky tests.

This example illustrates the additional complexity and manual intervention required when not using a tool like Testcontainers, which automates these aspects.

Spring Boot and Testcontainers

The integration of Testcontainers with Spring Boot is quite a potent way to facilitate comprehensive application testing, mainly when it comes to interactions with external systems or databases. This integration allows creating and managing containers dynamically during your tests while providing an isolated environment similar to your production setup.

Testcontainers integrates with JUnit, allowing us to define a test class that will start a container before the execution of any test. It is easy to use for integration tests communicating with backend services like MySQL, MongoDB, Redis, and so on.

Figure 10-2. *Testcontainers integration test*

Here's how we can utilize Testcontainers in a Spring Boot test.

Dependencies Setup

First, make sure the required dependencies are included in our Maven or Gradle setup is crucial:

For Maven:

```
<dependency>
            <groupId>org.springframework.boot</groupId>
            <artifactId>spring-boot-starter-test</artifactId>
            <scope>test</scope>
      </dependency>
      <dependency>
            <groupId>org.springframework.boot</groupId>
            <artifactId>spring-boot-testcontainers</artifactId>
            <scope>test</scope>
```

```
        </dependency>
        <dependency>
            <groupId>org.testcontainers</groupId>
            <artifactId>junit-jupiter</artifactId>
            <scope>test</scope>
</dependency>
```

For Gradle:

```
dependencies {
    testImplementation 'org.springframework.boot:spring-boot-
    starter-test'
    testImplementation 'org.springframework.boot:spring-boot-
    testcontainers'
    testImplementation 'org.testcontainers:junit-jupiter'
}
```

Alternatively, we can add dependencies using start.spring.io.

Figure 10-3. *Adding Testcontainers dependency*

Annotate Test Classes

Annotate your test classes with @SpringBootTest to enable Spring Boot
context loading for tests and @Testcontainers to activate Testcontainers
support.

```
@Testcontainers
@SpringBootTest
class DemoApplicationTests {
}
```

Container Initialization

Create container instances in your test classes using Testcontainers' utilities. For example, if you want to spin up an in-memory Redis cache instance:

```
@Testcontainers
@SpringBootTest
class DemoApplicationTests {
    @Container
    @ServiceConnection
    static RedisContainer container = new
    RedisContainer(RedisContainer.DEFAULT_IMAGE_NAME);
    @Test
    void myTest() {
        System.out.println(container.isRunning());
        System.out.println(container.getRedisURI());
    }
}
```

This code snippet demonstrates the integration of Testcontainers with Spring Boot, showcasing how to use a Redis container in a test scenario. Here's a breakdown of what each part of the code does:

- @Testcontainers: This annotation indicates that this test class will utilize Testcontainers. It allows us to manage the lifecycle of containers used within the test class.

- @SpringBootTest: Indicates that this is a Spring Boot test. It loads the complete application context and allows integration testing with Spring components.

- @Container: This annotation marks a field as a container Testcontainers manages. In this case, it declares a static field container of type RedisContainer. The RedisContainer is instantiated with the default Redis image name (RedisContainer. DEFAULT_IMAGE_NAME), which is pulled from the DockerHub Registry.

- @ServiceConncetion: Facilitates SpringBoot's autoconfiguration to dynamically enlist all the required properties. In the background, this annotation identifies the necessary properties from the container class or the Docker image name.

- myTest(): This is a test method annotated with @Test. Inside this method:

  - container.isRunning() Prints whether the Redis container is running or not.

  - container.getRedisURI() Retrieves and prints the URI of the running Redis container.

This code sets up a test class that utilizes Testcontainers to manage a Redis container. It demonstrates basic functionalities like checking if the container is running and retrieving its URI. This allows for integration testing, ensuring the application works correctly with a Redis instance managed by Testcontainers.

Here's how we can modify our previous example where we created a Redis cluster manually to use RedisContainer—a specialized container class for Redis (from testcontainers-java library).

```java
@SpringBootTest
@Testcontainers
public class EmployeeRepositoryIntegrationTest {
    @Container
    @ServiceConnection
    static RedisContainer redis = new
    RedisContainer(DockerImageName.parse("redis:latest"));
    @Autowired
    private EmployeeRepository employeeRepository;
    @Test
    public void testEmployeeRepository() {
        Employee employee = new Employee(1L, "John Doe",
        "Developer");
        employeeRepository.save(employee);
        Optional<Employee> foundEmployee = employeeRepository.
        findById(employee.getId());
        assertTrue(foundEmployee.isPresent(), "Employee should
        be found");
        assertEquals(employee.getName(), foundEmployee.get().
        getName(), "Employee names should match");
    }
}
```

This approach has several advantages:

- Testcontainers will automatically start a Redis container.

- No need for application-test.properties for containerized Redis instance.

- There is no need for a local Redis installation.

- You get a consistent and isolated test environment.

- Testcontainers automatically cleanups resources.

- Test suite works the same way in any environment (local, CI).

Summary

This chapter covers the basics of Testcontainers and using it with Java, with the focus on Spring Boot integration testing. It first explains what are the core concepts behind Testcontainers, its necessity, and its major features: support for diverse containers, integration with JUnit, and automatic resource management. Then, it goes into the implementation details, focusing on testing strategies for Spring Boot applications at unit and integration levels.

This chapter provides practical examples of setting up and using Testcontainers and demonstrates integration with Redis containers by detailing the required configuration steps. The main emphasis throughout the chapter is on the advantages of the Testcontainers way of doing things compared to traditional ways of testing—namely, in obtaining environment parity, portability, and efficient resource utilization. Practical implementation guidelines are also covered, such as dependency setup and proper annotation usage, to provide a complete understanding for developers on how to harness Testcontainers to have more reliable and maintainable integration tests.

CHAPTER 11

Docker Best Practices for Java Developers

Mastering Docker best practices and strategies for Java applications

Docker has become integral to modern Java development, providing consistent, portable, and efficient ways to package and deploy applications. Mastering the best practices involved in Docker is important for creating optimized, secure, and production-ready containerized applications for Java developers. This chapter shows how to use Docker effectively with Java applications, detailing techniques and strategies in important areas impacting container performance, security, and efficiency.

The practices discussed in this chapter address the common challenges that Java developers face when containerizing their applications, from managing build processes and runtime environments to optimizing resource usage and ensuring security. Best practices brought out from real-world experience and industry standards provide a strong foundation for the development of containerized Java applications that are both robust and maintainable.

© Ashish Choudhary 2025
A. Choudhary, *When Docker Meets Java*, https://doi.org/10.1007/979-8-8688-1300-9_11

Implementing Multistage Builds

Multistage build in Docker is a powerful technique that allows developers to create lean and secure images using multiple stages in one `Dockerfile`, each with its base image. We can significantly reduce the size of the final image and minimize its attack surface, making it more secure.

Understanding Multistage Builds

Separate build stages: A multistage Dockerfile is divided into multiple sections, each beginning with a `FROM` statement. These sections are called stages. We can have as many stages as we need, and each stage can use a different base image.

Building in layers: Each stage is built upon the layers from the previous stages. It means we can compile or build our application in an earlier stage using a base image that includes all our build dependencies and then copy only the artifacts we need into a later stage with a slimmer base image.

Artifact transfer between stages: We can copy artifacts from one stage to another using the `COPY --from=<stage>` command. It is typically used to move the compiled application from a build stage to a smaller runtime stage.

Discarding intermediate layers: Once the final image is built, all the intermediate layers created in the previous stages are discarded. This results in a much smaller final image containing what's needed to run the application.

Reducing image size and security footprint: Compiling and building the application in an initial stage and copying only the necessary artifacts to the final stage minimizes the size of the final image. Smaller images contain fewer components, translating to fewer potential vulnerabilities and a smaller attack surface.

Creating a Basic Multistage Build Dockerfile

Start with a build stage: Use a base image `maven:3.6.3-jdk-11` or another that suits our Java project. Add source code and any required build tools.

Compile the java code: Execute the build commands (`mvn clean package`, for instance) to compile the Java application.

Setup the runtime stage: Use a lighter base image `openjdk:11-jre-slim` for the runtime. Copy the compiled JAR or classes from the build stage.

Copying the compiled code to the runtime stage: Use the `COPY --from=build_stage /path/to/compiled/artifact /path/in/runtime/image` command to copy the necessary files.

Best Practices

Tips on organizing stages: Name each stage for clarity (e.g., `FROM maven:3.6.3-jdk-11 as builder`). Keep the build stage clean and focus only on what's necessary to compile the code.

Minimizing layers and cache usage: Minimize the number of layers by combining commands where possible. Leverage Docker's build cache by organizing commands of least to most likely to change.

Example

Stage 1. Build: Using Maven image, add source code, and run `mvn` package.

Stage 2. Runtime: Using the JRE image, copy the JAR file from the build stage.

Dockerfile structure:

```
# Build stage
FROM maven:3.6.3-jdk-11 as builder
WORKDIR /app
COPY . .
RUN mvn clean package
# Runtime stage
FROM openjdk:11-jre-slim
COPY --from=builder /app/target/myapp.jar /usr/local/lib/
myapp.jar
ENTRYPOINT ["java","-jar","/usr/local/lib/myapp.jar"]
```

Multistage builds are crucial for building light and secure Docker images for Java applications. Separation of the build and runtime environments can greatly reduce the size of the final image and minimize the security vulnerabilities that come with large and bloated images. That is a technique any serious Java developer should find invaluable in using Docker.

Creating Slimmer Container Images with Java Jlink

jlink, which was introduced in Java 9 as part of the Java Platform Module System, is a tool that allows users to create a custom Java runtime image containing only modules relevant to a particular application. Tailoring the runtime environment allows users to realize various important benefits, especially in terms of deployment in constrained environments, such as in containers.

Key Features and Benefits of jlink

- **Custom runtime images**: You can build a smaller, optimized Java runtime specifically to your application, including just the modules necessary and reducing runtime size as opposed to that of a normal Java Runtime Environment.

- **Performance optimization**: Application startup can be faster and reduce the number of system resources used; this is valuable in a cloud and microservices setup.

- **Enhanced security**: You reduce the surface area for security vulnerabilities by including only the modules that are required. Fewer modules mean fewer potential points of attack.

- **Modularization**: `jlink` works with the module system introduced in Java 9. This system allows for better encapsulation and more organized dependency management in Java applications.

Knowing jlink

- **Modules identification**: `jlink` works in terms of modules. Identify which modules are needed for your application. Analyze dependencies using tools such as `jdeps`.

- **Custom runtime creation**: Now, once you have identified which modules are needed, you create a runtime image by including those modules using the jlink command. That's a self-contained environment for running your application; no other installation of Java is needed to run it.

- **Command line usage**: jlink is used via the command line, where you specify the modules to include and other options, such as compression level or the output directory.

The following command creates a custom Java runtime image that includes only the specified Java platform modules and our modules, which is ideal for making small and efficient runtime environments for our Java applications.

```
jlink --module-path $JAVA_HOME/jmods:path/to/your/modules
--add-modules com.example.yourmodule --output path/to/output/
directory
```

In this command:

- --module-path: This option specifies the module path. The module path is a list of directories that jlink searches for module definitions. In this command, $JAVA_HOME/jmods the path to the jmods directory is in the Java home directory. The jmods directory contains definitions for the Java platform modules. And `path/ to/your/modules` path would replace this with the path to any additional modules we want to include in our runtime image that isn't part of the standard Java distribution.

- `--add-modules`: This option specifies the modules to add to the custom runtime image. In this case, `com. example.yourmodule` is the module name we want to include. We would replace `com.example.yourmodule` it with the actual name of the modules we have.

- `--output`: This specifies the path to the directory where the custom runtime image will be created. We would replace `path/to/output/directory` with the path where we want the runtime image to be saved.

The following diagram shows the critical steps involved in the `jlink` process.

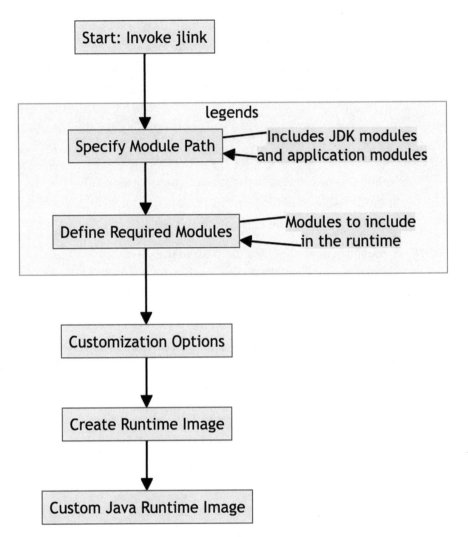

Figure 11-1. *jlink Java runtime image creation flow*

Use Cases for jlink

- **Containerized applications**: Especially designed for Docker and other container platforms where image size affects performance considerably as well as resource usage.

- **Creating minimal runtime environments**: Applications that only require a subset of the Java platform modules can create a runtime much smaller than the standard runtime. This is very helpful for microservices, serverless functions, or for any application where a small footprint is desirable.

- **IoT and embedded systems**: Useful in environments with limited resources, such as IoT devices or embedded systems.

- **Security**: Only necessary modules included, jlink reduces the surface area of security vulnerabilities. Applications are less prone to exploits that target modules that they do not even have.

- **Faster startup time**: A smaller runtime can contribute to faster application startup times, which is particularly advantageous for desktop applications and tools that benefit from quick launch times.

Step-by-Step Guide

Using Jlink in Dockerfile

- **Identify necessary modules:** Determine your application's required modules.

- **Create a Jlink Script:** Incorporate a script in your Dockerfile to execute Jlink with the identified modules.

- **Assemble the runtime image:** Use Jlink to create the custom runtime.

Selecting necessary Java modules

- Use tools like jdeps to analyze your application's module dependencies.

- Include these modules in your Jlink command in the runtime image.

Best Practices

- **Minimal module set:** Only include the necessary modules.

- **Compress the image:** Use Jlink's compression options to reduce the size further.

- **Layered Docker images:** Structure your Dockerfile to leverage Docker layer caching effectively.

Example

- **Scenario**: A simple Java application that uses HTTP and JSON processing.

- **Dockerfile setup**:

  - Start with a JDK image to compile the application and run Jlink.

  - Use Jlink to create a custom runtime including only the required modules (java.base, java.net.http, java.json).

  - Construct the final image using a minimal base, copying the custom runtime and application JAR.

- **Sample Dockerfile:**

```
# Compile Stage
FROM openjdk:11 as build
WORKDIR /app
COPY . .
RUN javac -d out --module-path lib --module-source-path
src $(find src -name "*.java")
RUN jlink --add-modules java.base,java.net.http,
java.json --output jre
# Final Stage
FROM alpine:latest
COPY --from=build /app/jre /opt/jre
COPY --from=build /app/out /app
ENTRYPOINT ["/opt/jre/bin/java", "-m", "com.myapp/com.
myapp.Main"]
```

Jlink significantly changes the way one dockerizes Java applications, enabling the creation of slimmer, more efficient container images. It is a powerful tool for Java developers, particularly in the context of Docker, where image size and security are paramount. Mastering Jlink enables developers to optimize their Java applications for modern cloud environments.

Using Distroless Base Images

The base image is very significant in defining the security, efficiency, and size of containerized applications. Distroless images have emerged with much popularity from Google. In particular, Java developers widely adopt it.

Understanding Distroless Images

Distroless images are minimalistic container images containing only the application and its runtime dependencies. They do not include package managers, shells, or other binaries typically found in a standard operating system distribution. For Java applications, a distroless image would typically include a JVM and the application's JAR file, nothing more.

Creating Distroless Java Image

Write a Dockerfile: Start with a base image that contains only a Java Runtime Environment (JRE).

```
FROM gcr.io/distroless/java17-debian12
COPY target/myapp.jar /app.jar
CMD ["app.jar"]
```

Build the image: Use Docker to build your image.

```
$ docker build -t my-java-app .
```

Run your container: Deploy your application.

```
$ docker run -d my-java-app
```

Benefits of Distroless Images

- **Enhanced security:** By removing unnecessary operating system components, the attack surface of the container is significantly reduced. Fewer components in the image mean fewer potential vulnerabilities.

- **Smaller image size:** Distroless images are minimalistic, making them smaller in size; they take less time to be pulled and pushed in the CI/CD pipeline. They use lesser storage spaces compared to other images. Smaller images accelerate the deployment time in orchestration systems such as Kubernetes.

- **Simplicity and maintenance:** With fewer components in the image, there's less need for patching and updates. Provides a clean and minimal environment for your application, ensuring consistency across different deployment environments.

Best Practices

- **Understand your application's dependencies**: Ensure all runtime dependencies are included in your image.

- **Debugging challenges**: With a shell or debugging tools, troubleshooting running containers can be more accessible. Consider using a debug version during the development phase.

- **Keep up with updates**: Regularly update the base image to ensure you have the latest security patches for the Java runtime.

Distroless images have a compelling approach in terms of deploying Java applications inside containers, balancing security, efficiency, and simplicity. Embracing distroless images means that developers and organizations reduce the risks of running large, complex container images in production while enjoying streamlined and efficient deployment processes. In the future, the industry will be more prone to distroless images with its trend towards minimalism in containerization.

Applying JVM Arguments and Resource Limits to Docker Containers

It is very important to optimize the JVM settings and container resource limits when running Java applications in Docker containers. Optimized configuration will ensure effective usage of resources, and consequently, application performance will increase without common issues like out-of-memory errors.

Importance of jvm Arguments and Resource Limits

JVM arguments: Customize the behavior of the JVM to suit specific needs, like garbage collection strategy, heap size, and other performance-related settings.

Resource limits in Docker: Define the maximum amount of CPU and memory resources a container can use, preventing any application from exhausting the host system's resources.

Setting memory limits: Use Docker's -m or --memory flag to set a memory limit.

Example: docker run -m 512m my-java-app caps the container at 512 MB of memory.

Setting cpu limits: Use --cpus to limit the number of CPU cores the container can use.

Example: docker run --cpus=2 my-java-app limits the application to 2 CPU cores.

Passing jvm Arguments in Docker

Use the JAVA_OPTS environment variable or pass arguments directly in the CMD or ENTRYPOINT in the Dockerfile.

```
docker run -e "JAVA_OPTS=-Xmx256m -Xms256m" my-java-app
```

Or we can include it in the Dockerfile.

```
ENTRYPOINT ["java", "-Xmx256m", "-Xms256m", "-jar",
"myapp.jar"]
```

Balancing Resources for Optimal Performance

- **Understand application needs**: Profile your application to understand its resource usage patterns.

- **Avoid over-allocation**: Don't allocate more resources than necessary, as it could starve other containers or processes.

- **Monitor and adjust**: Continuously monitor performance and adjust settings as needed.

Configuring Java Applications for Efficiency

Consider a scenario with a Java web application running in a Docker container. What do we need to take care of to get optimal performance from our web application? Per the current application load, we only need 700 MB of memory and one CPU core.

Inside the Dockerfile, we can set the memory limit to 1 GB and the CPU limit to 1 core. Even though the application needs ~700 MB of memory, we should keep some buffer in case there are spikes in the usage.

We should also configure JVM arguments for garbage collection and heap settings.

```
$docker build -t my-java-app .
$docker run -m 1g --cpus=1 -e "JAVA_OPTS=-Xmx700m -Xms700m -XX:
+UseG1GC" my-java-app
```

Tuning JVM settings and setting resource limits in Docker is essential for running Java applications efficiently and reliably in containerized environments. These configurations help manage application performance, ensure optimal use of resources, and maintain the stability of both the application and the host system. Regular monitoring and adjustments based on the application's behavior are essential to optimal performance.

Securing Docker Images

In containerization, Docker image security is paramount. With the widespread adoption of Docker in deploying applications, ensuring the security of Docker images is essential to protect against vulnerabilities that attackers could exploit.

Common Security Vulnerabilities

Although versatile, Docker is also vulnerable if not managed appropriately. This may offer attackers or hackers an entry point.

Common vulnerabilities include:

- **Outdated software and libraries**: Images containing outdated operating systems, libraries, or frameworks are vulnerable to known vulnerabilities.

- **Insecure configuration**: A misconfigured Dockerfile or container setting might expose the container to risk.

- **Embedded secrets**: Secrets hardcoded into images may cause unauthorized access.

- **Unnecessary packages**: The addition of unused software in images raises the attack surface.

Scanning for Vulnerabilities

- **Choose a scanning tool**: Tools like Clair, Trivy, Synk, or Docker's scanning feature can be used.

- **Integrate scanning into ci/cd pipeline**: Automate the scanning process during image build or deployment.

- **Review and address findings**: Analyze the report generated by the scanner and address the vulnerabilities identified.

Best Practices

- **Continuous monitoring**: Regularly scan images for vulnerabilities, even after deployment.

- **Dependency management**: Keep track of the dependencies used in your Docker images and update them regularly.

- **Minimize attack surface**: Use minimal base images and avoid installing unnecessary packages.

- **Non-root user**: Run your container as a non-root user to reduce the risk of a container breakout attack.

- **.dockerignore file**: Use a `.dockerignore` file to exclude unnecessary files and directories from your build context to prevent potential leaks of sensitive information.

- **Private registries and signed images**: Store images in trusted, private container registries with strong access controls. Use features like Docker Content Trust to sign images and verify their integrity and origin.

- **Implement the least privilege principle**: Ensure that files and executables within the Docker image have the least privileges necessary to run the application. Where possible, use read-only filesystems in your containers to prevent unwanted changes.

- **Securing application secrets**: Never hardcode sensitive information like passwords or API keys in Docker images. To manage sensitive information, use secret management tools like Docker Secrets, HashiCorp Vault, or environment variables injected at runtime.

- **Keeping host system secure**: Ensure the Docker daemon is securely configured. Keep the host system secure, as vulnerabilities in the host can affect all containers.

Securing of Docker images is an ongoing process that demands constant maintenance, vigilance, and best practices. By keeping up with vulnerabilities, maintaining the latest images, and minimizing attack surfaces, you can enhance your Docker deployments' security dramatically. The integration of security practices into the development and deployment pipeline is the way to ensure robust and secure containerized applications.

Choosing Maven vs. JDK vs. JRE Base Image

In the Docker ecosystem, choosing a base image is critical for building effective and efficient Java applications. Maven, JDK, and JRE images each serve different purposes. Understanding their differences and use cases is essential for optimal Docker image construction.

Differences between Maven, JDK, and JRE Images

- **Maven image**: Includes the Maven build tool and typically a JDK. Best for building Java applications from source.

- **JDK (Java Development Kit) image**: Contains the Java Runtime Environment (JRE), compilers, and tools to build Java-based applications. Required for compiling Java code.

- **JRE (Java Runtime Environment) image**: The runtime needed to execute a Java application. It does not contain the tools and compilers found in the JDK.

Pros and Cons

Image Type	Pros	Cons	Use Case
Maven Image	Convenient for building applications where Maven is the build tool - Often includes the JDK	Larger than JDK or JRE images, as it includes additional build tools	Building Java applications during development or in CI/CD pipelines
JDK Image	Essential for compiling Java code and includes necessary tools for development	Larger size compared to JRE images	Application development and any situation where Java code needs to be compiled

(*continued*)

Image Type	Pros	Cons	Use Case
JRE Image	Smaller size, focused on runtime only, and ideal for running Java applications	Cannot be used for compiling Java code or any development-related tasks	Running Java applications in production or any environment where code compilation is not required

Best Practices

- **Analyze your requirements**: Determine whether your application needs to be compiled or if it's only being run.

- **Consider the environment**: Use JDK images for development, CI/CD pipelines, and JRE images for production.

- **Size vs. functionality**: Balance the need for a smaller image size with the functionality required.

Example

- **Maven image**:

- **Scenario**: Building a Spring Boot application using Maven.

- **Dockerfile example**:

```
FROM maven:3.6-jdk-11 AS build
COPY src /usr/src/app/src
COPY pom.xml /usr/src/app
RUN mvn -f /usr/src/app/pom.xml clean package
```

- **JDK image**:

- **Scenario**: Compiling a Java application.

- **Dockerfile example**:

```
FROM openjdk:11-jdk
COPY . /usr/src/myapp
WORKDIR /usr/src/myapp
RUN javac Main.java
```

- **JRE image**:

- **Scenario**: Running a pre-compiled Java application.

- **Dockerfile example**:

```
FROM openjdk:11-jre-slim
COPY --from=build /usr/src/app/target/app.jar /usr/app/
ENTRYPOINT ["java", "-jar", "/usr/app/app.jar"]
```

It depends on the needs of your Java application in Docker. Maven images are most suitable for building scenarios that involve Maven, JDK images are best suited for development and compilation tasks, and JRE images are best optimized for running Java applications. Understanding and aligning these choices with your application requirements ensures efficiency, performance, and a streamlined development process.

Summary

This chapter is a comprehensive review of Docker best practices that are vital for Java developers in today's containerized environments. The chapter starts with multistage builds, which are advanced techniques for creating lean and secure Docker images. Isolating the build environment from the runtime environment greatly reduces the size of the final image but still keeps all the functionality needed; it shows how to structure Dockerfiles and handle artifacts between stages.

The discussion then moves on to Java runtime optimization using jlink, a powerful tool introduced in Java 9. This section shows developers how to create custom runtime images containing only the modules necessary for their applications. Not only does this targeted approach reduce container size, but it also improves security by minimizing the potential attack surface; it provides practical examples and best practices for module selection in real-world scenarios.

Moving on, the chapter on distroless base images covers the minimal container image containing just the application and its dependencies required at runtime. This proves to be very valuable for improving security and efficiency in removing unnecessary components, which results in a smaller, more secure, and easier-to-maintain and deploy container.

The chapter then goes into detail on JVM arguments and resource management, providing deep insight into the optimization of memory usage, CPU allocation, and garbage collection settings. The extensive coverage helps developers realize how resource allocation can be balanced for optimal performance and common pitfalls in containerized Java applications. The guidance provided ensures that applications run efficiently within their containerized environments while maintaining stability and reliability.

Finally, the chapter will summarize security considerations by offering a comprehensive examination of Docker image security best practices, including vulnerability scanning and secure configuration management, implementing principles of least privilege, continuous monitoring, and regular updating of containerized environments over the application life cycle. Combined, these practices deliver a complete approach to containerizing Java applications, enabling development teams to create solutions that are efficient, secure, and maintainable, without falling into common pitfalls in the implementation of Docker.

Index

© Ashish Choudhary 2025
A. Choudhary, *When Docker Meets Java*, https://doi.org/10.1007/979-8-8688-1300-9

Printed in the United States
by Baker & Taylor Publisher Services